CODES

OF

DESIRE

CODES
OF
DESIRE

ON THE NATURE OF REALITY

. . .

The Answer to Who, Where, and What

One Mountain, Many Paths: Oral Essays

Volume 21

DR. MARC GAFNI

Author: Gafni, Marc
Title: Codes of Desire
Identifiers: ISBN 979-8-88834-029-5 (electronic)
ISBN 979-8–88834–028–8 (paperback)

© 2025 Marc Gafni

Edited by Elena Maslova-Levin, Kathy Brownback, Talya Bloom, and Rachel Keune

World Philosophy and Religion Press,
in conjunction with

IP Integral Publishers

https://worldphilosophyandreligion.org

CONTENTS

CHAPTER 2   REWRITING THE SCRIPT OF DESIRE: FOR WOMEN, FOR LIFE, FOR FREEDOM— MAHSA AMINI DID NOT DIE IN VAIN

CHAPTER 3 FROM HOMO SAPIENS TO HOMO AMOR: RECLAIMING THE AUTHORSHIP AND AUTHORITY OVER OUR CODES OF DESIRE

CHAPTER 4 THE RESPONSE TO EXISTENTIAL AND CATASTROPHIC RISK IS THE DAWN OF DESIRE

CHAPTER 5   THE DEGRADATION OF DESIRE—DISCERNING ISRAEL & HAMAS CONFLICT: EVOLVING THE BATTLE OF GOOD & EVIL TO A HIGHER LEVEL OF CONSCIOUSNESS

CHAPTER 6   BARBIE, HAMAS, AND HOMO AMOR—FROM DEGRADED LOVE STORIES TO THE UNIVERSE: A LOVE STORY

CHAPTER 7   EROS AND GNOSIS AND ETHICS ARE ONE: REALITY IS EVOLVING CODES OF DESIRE

CHAPTER 8 COSMOEROTIC HUMANISM—TRANSITIONAL OBJECTS, EVOLVING CODES OF DESIRE, AND THE NEW HUMAN AND THE NEW HUMANITY

CHAPTER 9   CLARIFIED FIRST VALUES AND FIRST PRINCIPLES GENERATE RIGHTS AND RESPONSIBILITIES

CHAPTER 10   FROM VALUES TO RIGHTS

CHAPTER 11   IMPLICATIONS FOR SOCIAL STRUCTURE: IN DIALOGUE WITH DR. ZACHARY STEIN

EDITORIAL NOTE ABOUT AUTHORSHIP, EDITING, AND THE RADICAL CONTEXT FOR THIS SERIES

ORAL ESSAYS FROM THE ONE MOUNTAIN, MANY PATHS WEEKLY BROADCAST

This volume is part of the Oral Essays library, a series of lightly edited, compiled transcripts of oral teachings given by Dr. Marc Gafni and the late Barbara Marx Hubbard in their weekly online broadcast, *One Mountain, Many Paths,* which they co-founded in 2017. Originally called an "Evolutionary Church," *One Mountain, Many Paths* became a key venue for the articulation of an inspired and deeply grounded new Story of Value in response to the meta-crisis. Marc and Barbara—together with Zak Stein,[1] Kristina Kincaid, Ken Wilber, Sally Kempton, Lori Galperin, Aubrey Marcus and dozens of other thought-leaders over the years—began to articulate what they call a World Philosophy and World Religion[2] as a context for our diversity.

---

1   Zak, together with Ken Wilber, has been Marc's primary intellectual partner and an initiate lineage holder in CosmoErotic Humanism.

2   This project is grounded in four core organizational frameworks: 1) The Center for World Philosophy and Religion, co-founded by Marc Gafni, Zachary Stein, Sally Kempton, and Ken Wilber, and chaired over the years by John P. Mackey, Barbara Marx Hubbard, Aubrey Marcus, Gabrielle Anwar and Shareef Malnik, Carrie Kish and Adam Bellow, and Kathleen J. Brownback. 2) The Office for the Future, chaired by Stephanie Valcke and Ivan Bossyut. 3) The World Philosophy and Religion Press, founded and chaired by Aubrey Marcus, together with Marc Gafni and Zachary Stein. 4) The Foundation for Conscious Evolution, founded by Barbara Marx Hubbard and currently chaired by Peter Fiekowsky. For a complete list of key leadership, see the Office for the Future website, www. officeforthefuture.com.

Until Barbara's passing in 2019, she and Marc transmitted teachings together as evolutionary partners and "whole mates," weaving together insights and transmissions from their decades of practice, study, teaching, and activism into a synergy of wisdom, a grounded vision for future policy across all sectors of society.

Much of the Dharma material below comes directly from Marc, so it was originally all in quotation marks—but that looked a little odd. So per his suggestion we removed them, and the reader should consider the paragraphs on the next several pages as one extended quote from him. We are joyfully grateful to Marc for the clarity of his Dharma, the elegance and "second simplicity" of this language, and the mad, Outrageous Love with which he transmits his teachings.

Barbara and Marc called the mission of *One Mountain* "a Planetary Awakening in Evolutionary Love Through Unique Self Symphonies." We are an evolutionary community with a deeply grounded, radically alive, and "post-tragic" revolutionary spirit. We are activating a new humanity and awakening as a new species: *Homo amor*, the fulfillment of *Homo sapiens*.

One Mountain is committed to articulating a Story of Value that can become the ground for the new society that must be birthed in response to the meta-crisis. We recognize that we are living at a pivotal moment in history. In this "time between stories," the great moral imperative is to tell the new Story of Value. It is ours to do, personally and collectively, with great trembling and ecstatic joy.

FROM DOGMA TO DHARMA: ETERNAL AND EVOLVING FIRST PRINCIPLES AND FIRST VALUES

The teachings are grounded in decades of deep study across many wisdom traditions. Over the years, week by week, these teachings were incrementally developed within the framework of the *One Mountain, Many Paths* broadcast. We often refer to these teachings as *Dharma*.

This word was originally used in lineage traditions to refer to something like universal law. This is a crucial realization: just as there is universal law in mathematical value, there is also a sense of universal law in ethics and value.

Historically, Dharma often devolved into unchanging dogma. Evolution was ignored, and the natural process of Dharma evolution became disconnected from its deep, eternal context. The weakness of the word Dharma is that too often it did not include the evolving insights of the sciences, it confused local cultural truths with universal truths, and it used words like "eternal," as in "eternal Tao," as opposed to words like "evolution."

Eternal came to mean unchanging, and that kind of thinking often led to overly ethnocentric readings of Dharma. Local systems would claim their religious and cultural insights as immutable, which stood in the way of the emergence of a genuine world Story of Value that is real, inherent to Cosmos, and backed by the Universe—even as it is also always evolving.

Or, as we often say, "eternal value is evolving value. The eternal Tao is the evolving Tao."

We have shown that, emergent from profound insights in the "interior sciences," eternal does not mean unchanging in time; it means what we call the deeper Field of ErosValue that is beneath culture, geography, and history, which lives beneath all individual and collective values, and beneath time and space itself.

As such, we have gradually transitioned from the term Dharma to the term *Value*, in the sense of the Field of Value that lives beneath all values. This Field of Value discloses as First Principles and First Values embedded in a Story of Value.

Indeed, as the interior sciences knew and the exterior sciences imply, Reality arises in a Field of ErosValue in which an entire set of mathematical, musical, molecular, moral, and mystical values are the very ground of all being. That Field of Value is eternal—the true ground of the Good, True and Beautiful—even as it is evolving.

But of course, it is equally critical not just to talk about evolving value, but to ground the evolving value in its true nature, the eternal Field of First Principles and First Values, always reaching for ever more life, ever more love, ever more care, ever more depth, ever more uniqueness, ever more intimate communion, and ever more transformation.

As such, when we refer to the word Dharma, which still appears in these texts together with the word value, we refer to an evolving Dharma grounded in an *eternal and evolving* Field of Value. Indeed, eternity and evolution are two faces of the whole, opposites joined at the hip, that characterize the nature of our Cosmos in virtually all of its expressions.

It's in these terms that we ground a robust world philosophy that integrates the validated, leading-edge insights of premodern traditional wisdom, modern wisdom, and more recent postmodern insights, weaving them together into a new whole greater than the sum of its parts.

This new whole is a shared Story of Value rooted in First Principles and First Values that are both eternal and evolving.

These First Principles and First Values of Cosmos are woven together into a new Story of Value as a context for our diversity, a new Universe Story. This new Story gives us the best possible responses we have to the mystery, and to the great questions:

- Who am I? Who are we?
- Where am I? Where are we?
- What should I do? What should we do?

It is only through such a shared Universe Story—a narrative of identity and ethos as a context for our blessed diversity—that we can realize how what unites is so much greater than what divides us.

Only a new Story of Value will allow us to both respond to the meta-crisis and participate together in birthing the most true, good, and beautiful world that we already know is possible.

THIS ORAL ESSAYS SERIES IS AN ENTRYWAY TO THE GREAT LIBRARY OF COSMOEROTIC HUMANISM

This Oral Essays series is part of the overarching project of the Great Library at the Center for World Philosophy and Religion, led by Dr. Marc Gafni, together with Dr. Zak Stein. The aim of the Great Library project is to articulate a robust and comprehensive new Story of Value, CosmoErotic Humanism, in the form of dozens of well-researched and extensively footnoted academic works.

Our vision is to provide the philosophical framework that will be vital for navigating humanity through this time of immense crisis and transformation.

To begin your journey into CosmoErotic Humanism, we tenderly refer you to the book *First Principles and First Values*, co-authored by Marc Gafni, Zak Stein, and Ken Wilber, under the name David J. Temple. David J. Temple is a pseudonym created for enabling ongoing collaborative authorship at the Center for World Philosophy and Religion. The two primary authors behind David J. Temple are Marc Gafni and Zak Stein, and for different projects, specific writers will be named as part of the collaboration, such as Ken Wilber and others.

Three other volumes complete this introduction: *A Return to Eros*, by Marc Gafni and Kristina Kincaid; *Your Unique Self*, by Marc Gafni; and *Education in a Time between Worlds*, by Zak Stein.

We hope that the Oral Essays in the present volume, with their informal style of transmission, will serve as an allurement and entryway for you into the more formal books of the Great Library that provide the robust intellectual underpinnings of the new Story of Value.

A NOTE ABOUT THE EDITORS

This Oral Essays collection has been edited by students of the new Story of CosmoErotic Humanism. Each of us has actively participated in *One Mountain, Many Paths*, and most of us have been in deep "Holy of Holies" study with Dr. Marc Gafni for many years.

We have been privileged to find ourselves well-versed in the teachings, and even emerging as lineage-holders of CosmoErotic Humanism.[3]

We view this editing project as a privilege and a deep practice of study and clarification. We experience ourselves as a *mystical editing society*, frequently meeting and conversing together about the content—the depth of knowledge and wisdom offered here—as well as the technical intricacies involved with publishing a beautiful and coherent series of books. In so doing, we function as a "Unique Self Symphony," which itself is a Dharmic

---

3 CosmoErotic Humanism is a world philosophical movement aimed at reconstructing the collapse of value at the core of global culture. Much like Romanticism or Existentialism, CosmoErotic Humanism is not merely a theory but a movement that changes the very mood of Reality. It is an invitation to participate in evolving the source code of consciousness and culture towards a cosmocentric *ethos* for a planetary civilization.

The term CosmoErotic Humanism, initially coined by Dr. Gafni and colleagues, points to a complex, multi-faceted, layered, and nuanced evolutionary set of insights that has evolved over decades of intensive research, teaching, and spiritual practice from deep within a wide range of wisdom traditions (including the Wisdom of Solomon lineage tradition, Bodhisattva Buddhism, and Kashmir Shaivism), as well as multiple disciplines including complexity theory, chaos theory, emergence theory, molecular biology, and the more classical disciplines of the humanities.

The seeds of CosmoErotic Humanism were planted with Dr. Marc Gafni's work on a two-volume, 1,000-page opus called *Radical Kabbalah* (Integral Publishers, 2012). This scholarly work, sourced from deep study within the esoteric lineage texts of the Wisdom of Solomon, points to a non-dual, or acosmic, realization which—unlike the prevailing conceptualization of non-duality—does not efface the human being; rather, it is highly humanistic in its nature. The next step in the evolution of CosmoErotic Humanism was the insight that all of Reality is evolving Eros, which lives in, as, and through the human being.

A failure of Eros leads inexorably to the creation of narratives of "pseudo-eros." CosmoErotic Humanism is a response to the modern mental and social breakdown sourced in the proliferation of multiple forms of pseudo-eros and its broken narratives, such as rivalrous conflict governed by win/lose metrics and the dogmatic denial of intrinsic value in Cosmos, which together generate our current "global intimacy disorder."

term that connotes an omni-considerate collaboration between realized Unique Selves synergizing our unique gifts into a new emergence greater than the sum of the parts. Even as we worked diligently to standardize our editing styles, meeting on a weekly basis to debate the nuances of phrasing, we also operated from within a deep appreciation of the unique style that each editor brought to his or her work. As such, the reader might notice some variation in editing style among the books.

Please note that Dr. Marc Gafni has not reviewed these edited Oral Essays, as he is deeply engaged in writing the formal books of the Great Library. But he has been generous in responding to questions and providing overall guidance in the project. Overall, as Marc's students and students of the Dharma, we have made it a key project at the Center to publish these pieces of work relatively independently.

OUR UNIQUE ORAL-ESSAY EDITING STYLE PRESERVES THE ENERGY OF THE ORIGINAL TRANSMISSION

Dr. Marc Gafni is a uniquely gifted teacher whose oral transmission is imbued with a quality that has proven transformative for his students. Many of us feel mystically transformed by both the content and the underlying energy of the transmission style. Therefore, as we like to say, *trust the magic ways the Dharma comes through your unique understanding!*

As Marc's empowered students, colleagues, and beloved friends, we have a deep knowing that these teachings are vital for the survival and thriving of humanity as we know it, and we recognize the importance of publishing his teachings in a written format that will be accessible by future generations. At the same time, we sought to preserve the Eros of the original oral transmission with all of its nuance, power, and depth. Our intention in the editing process, to the greatest extent possible, has been to keep these spoken artifacts intact in order to maintain the flow of the original transmission. We have therefore chosen not to engage in intensive formal editing, as we found that doing so resulted in the loss of the energetic transmission that is so key to fully receiving the Dharma.

After experimenting with many ways to present these texts, we developed a specific way of laying out the text on the page. Marc, in collaboration with Zak Stein and Russian intellectual/artist Elena Maslova-Levin—and ultimately all of the editors, through many conversations—developed a unique, artistic presentation of the text, using bolding, italics, bullet points, and other stylistic features which together serve to accentuate the immediacy of the oral transmission.

As part of this editing style, intended to preserve the integrity of the original transmission, we have refrained from removing the frequent recapitulations of key themes. We found that each recapitulation contributes something vital to the rhythm and music beneath the words, like the beating drum of our hearts. These recapitulations not only review previous material but also add important new emphases, perspectives, and elements of the new Story of Value. We ask for your patience as a reader to trust the rhythm of these texts, and we trust you as a reader to have the depth and steadiness to find your way through.

KEY COMPONENTS: LINK TO THE ORIGINAL BROADCAST, EVOLUTIONARY LOVE CODES AND PRAYER

To supplement the written word, each episode includes a QR code linking to the original broadcast on YouTube, as well as occasional links to featured songs and video clips.

Each episode also centers around an "Evolutionary Love Code," formulated by Marc. These codes are part of the ongoing articulation and distillation of the Dharma as it unfolds and emerges, week by week, over the course of many years, through the mystical process we call Outrageous Love or Evolutionary Love.

Another core component of the *One Mountain, Many Paths* episodes is what Marc and Barbara called "Evolutionary Prayer." Prayer is experienced in *One Mountain* not in the old fundamentalist sense of a "cosmic vending-machine god" who is alienated from Cosmos. Marc refers to this as the "god you do not and should not believe in"—and he often adds, "the god you don't believe in does not exist."

GOD IS THE INFINITE INTIMATE

In fact, in the Dharma of CosmoErotic Humanism, a new name for God has emerged: the "Infinite Intimate," who appears in first-, second-, and third-person expressions. Marc first shared this name as he heard it whispered in 2023, although earlier intimations and formulations of the name appeared as early as 2010.

In first person, God is infinitely alive and as intimate as our own first-person experience.

In second person, God is the infinitely intimate Personhood of Cosmos that knows our name and holds us—the God about whom we say, *whenever we fall, we fall into Her hands.* This is the God who is our Beloved, Father, Mother, Lover, and Evolutionary Partner.

Finally, in third person, God inheres in all of the First Principles and First Values of Cosmos, and in the laws of science (both interior and exterior) that govern manifest Reality.

Therefore, we have a realization of God as not only the Infinity of Power but also the Infinity of Intimacy.

In *One Mountain, Many Paths*, we are reclaiming prayer at a higher level of consciousness. And we are reclaiming prayer as deep, alive, loving, and intimate conversations with God as the Infinite Intimate who knows our name.

THE INVITATION

We invite you to find your way into this revolution. Each one of our Unique Selves and unique gifts are desperately needed as we co-create this new Story of Value together, as part of the covenant between generations, for the sake of the whole.

Let's *play a larger game* and evolve the very source code of consciousness and culture together.

With mad love,

The Editors

LOVE OR DIE

LOCATING OURSELVES: ARTICULATING THE ESSENTIAL CONTEXT FOR THE ONE MOUNTAIN, MANY PATHS ORAL ESSAYS

SETTING OUR INTENTION

Intention setting is everything.

We're here—as da Vinci was with his cohort in the Renaissance—**to play a larger game, to participate in the evolution of love, which is to tell the new Story of Value rooted in First Principles and First Values.**

- Our intention is to recognize the critical historical juncture in which we find ourselves.
- Our intention is to take our seat at the table of history and to say, *we take responsibility for this.*
- Our intention is to participate as revolutionaries for the sake of the whole.

What we're here to do is revolution; revolution for the sake of the evolution of love.

It's a revolution for the sake of the trillions of unborn lives that will not manifest:

- The unborn loves
- The unborn creativity
- The unborn goodness
- The unborn truth
- The unborn beauty

All of it looks to us.

Not because we're engaged in grandiosity. Not at all!

- We're trembling before She.
- We're trembling with joy at the privilege.
- We're trembling with joy at the responsibility.
- We're trembling with joy at the Possibility of Possibility.
- We have to enact a new Story in this moment of time. Because it is only a new Story that can change the vector of history.

The most revolutionary act that we can do—the greatest moral imperative of this time—**is to articulate a new Story at this time between worlds and this time between stories.**

Story is not made up, as postmodernity suggests. **We all live in inescapable frameworks; our framework is the story we live in.** Right now, Reality lives according to win/lose metrics, a story that is generating existential risk. **We need to change that story.**

When we change that story, when we tell a new Story—not a made-up story, but a new Story of Value, rooted in First Principles and First Values—**then it all changes.**

We need to participate in the evolution of the source code of consciousness and culture, which is the evolution of love.

It's the most important, exciting, evolutionary, revolutionary act that we can do to alleviate suffering: to be lovers.

Like Rumi, the great poet of Sufism, we have to be "mad lovers," because it's the only sanity.

To be mad lovers is to see around the corner, to not be so obsessed with the details of the contractions of my life.

Let me see bigger.

Let me take complete care of myself in every possible way, let me completely attend to those in my circle of intimacy and influence, and then—*let me expand my circle.*

That's what we're here for.

- Our intention is to participate in the *LoveForce*, the *LoveIntelligence*, the *LoveBeauty*, the *LoveDesire* that literally animates Cosmos all the way up and all the way down.
- Our intention is to participate in the evolution of love.

[*In the next few pages we will cover some key concepts which are essential to locating ourselves and setting the context for all the One Mountain, Many Paths Oral Essays. —Eds.*]

OVERVIEW: EROS IS NO LONGER A LUXURY—IT'S LOVE OR DIE

Eros is life.

The failure of Eros destroys life.

Our lack of Eros is poised to destroy the world.

All civilizations have fallen because the stories that they lived in were, in some sense, stories based on rivalrous conflict governed by win/lose metrics. Every civilization was weakened by interior polarization caused by the lack of a shared Story of Value.

We now have a global civilization, but we haven't created a shared Story of Value.

We haven't solved the generator functions that caused all civilizations to fall. Our global civilization has exponential technologies and extraction models depleting the Earth of resources that took billions of years to create, which is going to lead to a civilizational collapse.

Existential risk is risk to our very existence.

The choice is clear: love or die.

It's that simple.

Eros is no longer a luxury. It is an absolute necessity for the survival of the individual and the planet.

In the last half a century, modern psychology has documented an age-old truth: a fully nourished baby who is not held in loving arms will die.

So too, our world, both personal and global—even with all the resources of intelligence and technology at our disposal—will die without being held in love, in the embrace of Eros.

We must embrace a personal path of love and a global politics of love.

Not ordinary love. Not love which is "mere human sentiment," but Eros, or what we sometimes call Outrageous Love, which is the heart of existence itself.

We live in a world of outrageous pain.

The only response is Outrageous Love.

WHAT IS EROS?

Eros is the experience of radical aliveness, moving towards, seeking, desiring ever deeper contact and ever greater wholeness.[4] Eros is the core fabric of Reality's being and the motivational architecture of Reality's becoming.

Eros is what animates the evolutionary impulse itself, from the very inception of Cosmos all the way to our very selves, who awaken to the realization that the evolutionary impulse throbs uniquely in each of us.

The realization of human awakening and transformation that lies at the core of the interior sciences is the invitation—or even the urgent and desperate demand—of a madly loving Cosmos animated by infinities of power and infinities of intimacy.

The demand—the desperate invitation, the plea, the tender and fierce command of Cosmos that lives inside every human being—is to awaken: to awaken to our true nature as unique incarnations of Eros and Ethos that are needed and desperately desired by All-That-Is. Said slightly differently: Reality is Eros. Or: God is Eros.

The failure of Eros destroys life. The collapse of Eros is always the hidden (or not so hidden) root cause for the collapse of ethics.

This is true both personally and collectively. We live in a moment of a worldwide and personal collapse of Eros. Our lack of Eros is poised to destroy

---

4 We define Eros through what we refer to as the Eros equation (one of a series of what we call interior science equations):

> *Eros = Radical Aliveness x Desiring (Growing + Seeking) x Deeper Contact x Greater Wholeness x Self Actualization/Self Transcendence (Creation [Destruction])*

There are good reasons for the formal language of the interior science equations in these writings, and the reader is invited to explore them on their own, in particular, in our work, David J. Temple, *First Principles and First Values: Forty-Two Propositions on CosmoErotic Humanism, the Meta-Crisis, and the World to Come* (World Philosophy and Religion, 2024).

the world. Humanity is currently experiencing what has come to be known as existential risk, a risk to our very existence, or what I will refer to as the Second Shock of Existence.

EXISTENTIAL RISK: THE SECOND SHOCK OF EXISTENCE

The first shock of existence is the death of the human being—the realization that we will die, which dawns in human consciousness at the beginning of history. We are not talking about the biological fact of death but the *existential* realization of death. Although the interior sciences disclose that death is a portal between two days (there is vast empirical,[5] philosophical,[6] and anthro-ontological evidence[7] for the continuity of consciousness[8]), death is also, in our own direct surface experience, a stark end. And that is obviously not a bug but a feature in the system.

---

5   We refer to evidence gathered by the most serious of researchers, beginning with Henry and Edith Sedgwick at Cambridge University and William James at Harvard University, and continuing in highly rigorous form for the last 150 years, as recapitulated by Whiteheadian scholar David Ray Griffin in multiple volumes. See also, for example, Dean Radin, *Real Magic: Unlocking Your Natural Psychic Abilities to Create Everyday Miracles* (Potter/TenSpeed/Harmony, 2018), *The Conscious Universe: The Scientific Truth of Psychic Phenomena* (HarperCollins, 2010), and other books. Or see the earlier classic by Frederic William Henry Myers, *Human Personality and Its Survival of Bodily Death* (Longmans, Green, 1907).

6   This requires a cogent analysis of materialism and dualism, and the introduction of the far more cogent third possibility which we have called "pan-interiority."

7   We discuss Anthro-Ontology in some depth in *First Principles and First Values*, and see also the fuller conversation in David J. Temple, *First Principles and First Values: Towards an Evolving Perennialism: Introducing the Anthro-Ontological Method*—both published by World Philosophy and Religion Press, in Conjunction with Integral Publishers. For now, we will simply define it as an "innate and clear interior gnosis directly available to the human being."

8   See Dr. Marc Gafni and Dr. Zachary Stein's essay in preparation, "Beyond Death: Anthro-Ontology, Philosophy, and Empiricism." This essay is slated to appear in the book *Towards a World Religion: Homo Amor Essays.* The essay is also the ground for a larger book by the same authors, *Twelve Portals to Life Beyond Death: Responding to the Second Shock of Existence,* in which we discuss three forms of material: the empirical, the philosophical, and the anthro-ontological, and show how each form discredits the notion of death as the end.

Our first-person experience is that death ends this life. It is not the *totality* of our experience if we go deeper inside, but it is obviously intended to be the central, potent, and painful dimension of every human life. Indeed, as Ernest Becker potently reminded us, the denial of death is at our peril.

All the stories and all the plotlines and all the threads of living end at that moment. Whatever happens beyond, we have an actual experience of ending. **Paradoxically, that ending, the experience of the finality of mortality, is what presses us into life.** From the implicit demand of the first shock of existence, human beings were activated and pressed into creative emergence, and what emerged was all of human culture, both interior and exterior.

The second shock of existence is the realization of the potential death of all humanity. After all the stages of human history—matter, life, and mind in all of their stages of evolutionary unfolding—we have come to this place in the evolution of humanity, in which the gap between our exponentially expanding exterior technologies and our stalled (or even regressing) interior technologies of value has created dire catastrophic and existential risks.

This gap generates extraction models and exponential growth curves, rivalrous conflicts based on win/lose metrics, tragedies of the commons, and multipolar traps, in which everyone has to keep producing to the *n*th degree, including weaponized exponential threats to our very existence because we are afraid that the other parties are going to do it and not be transparent—hide it from us and then dominate us.

GENERATOR FUNCTIONS FOR EXISTENTIAL RISK

Let's outline clearly the main *generator functions for existential risk*.

Rivalrous conflicts governed by zero-sum, win/lose metrics. Rivalrous conflicts generate extraction models at the core of the economic system and exponential growth curves. Both of these drive and are driven by a contrived system of artificially manufactured desires and needs, delivered into culture by ever more precise forms of micro-targeting to individuals and groups through the ever more immersive environment of the internet.

Next, rivalrous conflicts and exponential growth curves animated by win/lose metrics generate **complicated, fragile world systems** highly vulnerable to myriad forms of collapse. Fragile local systems are made exponentially more fragile on a global level by our inability to meet global challenges with social, legal, political, economic, and ethical infrastructures that remain largely local.

All of this is a direct result of the failure to develop more adequate interior technologies that would be sufficiently compelling to displace "rivalrous conflict governed by win/lose metrics" as the motivational architecture for the human life world.

This failure has led to the conditions that will cause the implosion of systems that are already and quite literally on the brink of collapsing themselves. That's what we mean by the *second shock of existence*.

To recapitulate: the second shock of existence is not the death of the human being, but the potential death of humanity.

It is the *Death Star* moment of our species.

THE DECONSTRUCTION OF INTRINSIC VALUE

We stand in this moment poised between utopia and dystopia, at a time between worlds and a time between stories. We need a new Story of Value, eternal yet evolving, rooted in First Principles and First Values, which would become a universal grammar of value and a context for our diversity.

This is exactly what the Renaissance was. It was a time between worlds and a time between stories. In the Renaissance, we had been recently challenged by the Black Death, a pandemic that swept across Europe. The Black Death destroyed between a third to half of Europe and a huge part of

Asia. People died horrifically, brutally, in the streets. They had no idea how to meet this challenge, and so, in response to the Black Death, da Vinci and Ficino and their cohorts understood that they had to tell a new Story of Value.

That story was the story of modernity. Did they get it right?

- They got part of it right, which birthed, to use Jürgen Habermas' phrase, "the dignities of modernity," such as new ways of gathering information and universal human rights.
- But they also deconstructed the source of Value. They lost the basis for the Good, the True, and the Beautiful.

The basis used to be divine revelation: *God told us*. But this claim was owned by religion, and every religion began to overreach and over-claim. The revelation was thus often mediated through cultural categories and wasn't fully accurate.

Modernity threw out revelation, but was unable to establish a new basis for value.

Value was just assumed to be real. As it says in the founding document of the American Revolution: *We hold these truths to be self-evident*—that is, *we don't really have a basis for value; we just take it as a given.*

In other words, modernity took out a loan of social capital from the traditional world. The source of value was never worked out.

And then, gradually, value began to collapse.

- The Universe Story began to collapse.
- The belief that the Good, the True, and the Beautiful are real began to collapse.
- The belief that Love is real began to collapse.

As Bertrand Russell is reported to have said, "I cannot see how to refute the arguments for the subjectivity of ethical values, but I find myself incapable of believing that all that is wrong with wanton cruelty is that I do not like it."

What do you do if you grew up in a world in which value is not real? A world without a source of value, without a Universe Story, without a story of human identity, without a story of desire, without a narrative of power?

In the words of W.B. Yeats, *the center does not hold.*

- You have a collapse at the very center of society, because you no longer have Eros.
- You no longer have a Reality in which value is real, and so you have this lingering sense of emptiness.
- You have a complete collapse at the very center.
- We become *the hollow men and the stuffed men,* gesture without form.

And that's the source of our current existential risk.

THE DEEPER ROOT CAUSE OF THE META-CRISIS: A GLOBAL INTIMACY DISORDER

Above, I have outlined the major generator functions of existential risk. But there is a deeper cause for the existential risk that lurks underneath the rivalrous conflict governed by win/lose metrics and the fragile systems they engender.

And we cannot take the Death Star down without discerning and addressing this. We have already alluded to this root cause above, but at this point we need to make it more explicit so that, from this context, the adequate root response will become clear.

Modernity threw out the revelation, but was unable to establish a new basis for value.

This ostensibly surprising statement can be understood in a few simple steps:

1. All of the catastrophic and existential risk challenges we face are global: from climate change to artificial intelligence, pandemics, systems collapse, and exponential arms races.
2. Every global challenge self-evidently requires a global solution.
3. Global solutions can only be implemented with global co-ordination.
4. Global co-ordination is impossible without global coherence.
5. Global coherence is only possible if there is a global resonance between the parts.
6. Global resonance is only possible if we have global intimacy.

ONLY A SHARED STORY OF VALUE CAN GENERATE GLOBAL INTIMACY

Global intimacy—just like intimacy in a couple—is only possible when there is a shared story.

Not just a shared history, but a shared Story of Value.

- It is only a shared global story that can generate a new emergent quality of intimacy: global intimacy.
- A shared Story of Value must be rooted in shared ordinating values, or what we have called evolving First Values and First Principles.
- Intimacy requires a shared grammar of value as a matrix for a shared Story of Value.

The global intimacy disorder is the root cause for existential risk. The global intimacy disorder underlies the core generator functions for existential risk.

The global intimacy disorder is rooted in the failure to experience ourselves in a field of shared intrinsic value. This failure derives from the deconstruction of value.

Indeed, it is wholly accurate to say that **the root cause of the two generator functions of existential risk is the failed story of intrinsic value, or what we might also call the breakdown of Eros.**

1. The first generator function is **the success story**. Our modern success story is rivalrous conflict governed by win/lose metrics, which violates all the terms of the Intimacy Equation: there is no shared identity and no mutuality of recognition, feeling, value or purpose, and instead of *relative* otherness, there is *alienated* otherness. Such a story generates complicated fragile systems with no allurement or intimacy between the parts, systems which optimize for efficiency (as an expression of win/lose metrics) and not for resiliency and life.

2. The second generator function is **the deconstruction of intrinsic value** itself. The deconstruction of value is the sense that human value does not participate in the intrinsic value of the Real, for the Real is dogmatically declared to have no intrinsic value. Thus, there is no shared identity between the interior of the human being and Reality. There is no common participation in a field of shared intrinsic value. Instead of being intimate with value, we are alienated from value. And only intrinsic value can arouse will: political, moral, and social will.

To sum up, without a shared grammar of value there is no global intimacy, and therefore no global coherence, and no global coordination in response to catastrophic and existential risk, which means, put simply, there will be, quite literally, no future.

HEALING THE GLOBAL INTIMACY DISORDER
REQUIRES THE EVOLUTION OF INTIMACY

But we are not hopeless. On the contrary, we are filled with great hope. Hope is a memory of the future. That memory of the future *is* the direct hit that takes down the Death Star, the culture of death. **The direct hit must be**—as it has always been in history—**the emergence of a new stage of evolution**.

Crisis is an evolutionary driver, and every crisis is, at its core, a crisis of intimacy: from the oxygen crisis of the single cells dying which generated multicellular life at the dawn of existence, to the existential risk in this very moment.[9]

> *The direct hit is therefore structurally self-evident: the evolution of intimacy itself.*

What is intimacy, as a structure of Cosmos all the way down and all the way up the evolutionary chain? We engage this inquiry in depth in other writings, but for now we will simply adduce what we have called the "Intimacy Equation":

Intimacy = shared identity in the context of [relative] otherness x mutuality of recognition x mutuality of pathos x mutuality of value x mutuality of purpose

Intimacy is about the capacity of parts to generate a *shared identity* while retaining their otherness, or distinct identity. This requires multiple mutualities, including recognition, pathos (or feeling), value, and purpose. The parts must recognize and feel each other, even as they share value and purpose. But all of this must lead to intimate union—and not pathological

---

9 We demonstrate this principle in some depth in the multi-volume series, *The Universe: A Love Story* (forthcoming) (https://worldphilosophyandreligion.org/early-ontologies), *The Intimate Universe: Global Intimacy Disorder as Cause for Global Action Paralysis* (forthcoming), and in other writings of CosmoErotic Humanism.

fusion, where the distinct identity of the parts disappears—like subatomic particles that successfully become an atom, or two people who successfully become a couple.

THE DECONSTRUCTION OF VALUE IS THE DECONSTRUCTION OF INTIMACY

We have identified the global intimacy disorder as the root cause of the existential risk. But the underlying ultimate failure of intimacy is the deconstruction of value itself.

The deconstruction of value means that human value does not participate in any sense of intrinsic value of the Real. This is not about individual *values,* but about *the Field of Value* that underlies all of them. **When the human being**—moved, often sincerely or even nobly, by myriad cultural, historical, and psychological confusions—**claims to have stepped out of the Field of Value, then intimacy itself is deconstructed.**

The deconstruction of value is the deconstruction of intimacy.

In the absence of a shared Story of Value, a story that is an authentic expression of Reality's Eros, a story rooted in *pseudo-Eros* takes center stage and becomes the generator function for existential risk. Our modern pseudo-Eros story is *rivalrous conflict governed by win/lose metrics.* Such a story catalyzes in its wake the second generator function of existential risk: *complicated fragile systems with no allurement or intimacy between the parts.* It is in that sense that we have argued that the first generator function for existential risk is the success story.

- The failure of intimacy is precisely the impotent experience that there is no shared identity between the interior of the human being and Reality. **There is no shared identity in the sense of any kind of common participation in a field of shared intrinsic value.**
- **But only a shared Story of Value can arouse the global will**

required to engage catastrophic and existential risk. For it is only global political, moral, and social will—and we can even say *erotic* will—that can generate the most Good, True and Beautiful world that we have always known is possible.

THE EVOLUTION OF LOVE IS THE TELLING OF A NEW STORY

Coupled with the Intimacy Equation is the scientifically grounded realization, in both the exterior and interior sciences, that Reality is a progressive deepening of intimacies, or, said slightly differently:

Reality is Evolution. Evolution is the evolution of intimacy.

- The evolution of intimacy requires—both personally and collectively—a deeper, more accurate discernment of the nature of our universe, ourselves, and our beloveds.
- This new discernment generates a new global Story of Value.
- The new global Story of Value generates an emergent, heretofore unseen global intimacy and heals the global intimacy disorder.

The new Story of Value is the direct hit that takes down the Death Star and replaces it with the hope that invokes the memory of our best future.

Global intimacy facilitates global coherence, which facilitates global coordination, which activates the possibility of our creative and effectively coordinated global responses to the global meta-crisis in its entirety and its specific expressions.

To solve Bertrand Russell's challenge—the apparent argument for the subjectivity of ethical values—**we have to reground value theory in eternal yet evolving First Principles and First Values, and articulate a new Story of Value.**

This is what we call CosmoErotic Humanism.

CosmoErotic Humanism—together with other emergent strands—**needs to become the ground of a world religion as a context for our diversity**. We need religion, even as we need science, to articulate a shared global grammar of value.

As we said at the beginning, our choice is simple: love or die.

- To love means to participate in the evolution of love, which is the evolution of the human Story of Value.
- To love means to evolve and activate a new cultural enlightenment—rooted in a new narrative of identity, a new narrative of value, a new narrative of intimate communion, a new narrative of desire, a new narrative of power—all of which will birth new narratives of economics and politics.
- The evolution of love is the telling of a new Story.

The new Story that must be told is a love story, for in fact that is the deepest truth of Reality, rooted in the best exterior and interior sciences, that we have at this moment in time:

- Reality is not merely a fact. Reality is a story.
- Reality is not an ordinary story. Reality is a love story.
- Reality is not an ordinary love story. Reality is an Outrageous Love Story.

Story doesn't mean it's *made-up*.

It means doing the hard work of integrating the validated insights of the traditional world, the modern world, and the postmodern world.

This is the intention at the heart of telling the new Story of CosmoErotic Humanism.

CODES OF DESIRE: AN OVERVIEW

REALITY IS CODED WITH DESIRE

Reality is not empty or blind. Reality is animated by plotlines. These are the plotlines of evolution. The plotlines of evolution are Reality's codes of desire. Indeed, evolution at its very core is a code of desire.

Simply said: Reality is coded with desire. And Reality's desire is not merely generic. Reality's desire has *telos*, or purpose.

There is not only an unimaginable potency to Reality's desire; there is also an inherent precision.

Reality's desire is for value. Reality's codes of desire reach for ever more value. Eros generates ever more value.

Reality is animated by Eros, which itself is the animating force and motivational architecture of evolution. Eros desires ever more value. This desire is the inherent nature of evolution itself. At core, one might say that there is no split between Eros and value.

Eros is the great value of Cosmos, and value itself is suffused with Eros.

As such, it is appropriate and accurate to link the words into one phrase, ErosValue.

ErosValue and ErosDesire are the very heart of Reality itself.

The core ErosValue of Reality is the desire for ever more life, for ever greater depths of aliveness in all its forms.

Life and aliveness include:

- Ever deeper contact
- Ever greater wholeness
- Ever greater uniqueness
- Ever greater capacity for intimacy
- Ever greater goodness, truth, and beauty
- Ever greater consciousness
- Ever greater creativity
- Ever greater transformation
- Ever greater harmony, justice, and fairness

And more.

Each of these are First Principles and First Values of Reality. They are Reality's plotlines.

In other words, Reality's plotlines are the evolution of Her values.

REALITY'S VALUE IS BOTH ETERNAL AND EVOLVING

Value is inherent and eternal. And value is also evolving.

Value is eternal, but not in the sense of being preordained, everlasting, or unchanging.

Rather, as Wittgenstein—one of the great modern logical positivists points out, eternity does not mean everlasting time, but that which is beneath time.

There is no contradiction between value being both eternal and evolving.

As such, we realize that the eternal value is evolving.

Said somewhat differently: *The Eternal Tao is the Evolving Tao.*

Eternal value and evolving value are the core nature of Reality's story.

REALITY IS A FIELD OF *EROSVALUE* IN WHICH DEEPER VALUE AND GREATER WHOLENESS EMERGE FROM THE DIALECTICAL PLAY OF DIVERSE VALUES

Reality is a Field of *Eros Value*:

- Eros is "the experience of radical aliveness desiring ever deeper contact and ever greater wholeness."
- Wholeness means value.
- More wholeness means more value.
- More value means *more* of the same value, as well as *deeper versions* of the same Value.
- Deeper value also emerges from the higher weave of diverse values into a larger whole. For example, the dialectical play between the two diverse values of autonomy [freedom] and communion [intimacy] generates new value. **From this dialectical play, from this higher weave of autonomy and communion, a new wholeness is born.**

HUMAN BEINGS PARTICIPATE IN THE DESIRE OF REALITY FOR EVER GREATER VALUE

Reality is desire. And Reality's desire is always for more value. Reality's desire is always for ever evolving Value.

Human beings are participatory in Reality. Like all of Reality, the plotlines of our lives are mapped by our codes of desire.

Our codes of desire participate in the wider Field of Desire. Our codes of desire are unique human incarnations of the wider Field of Desire.

The evolution of Reality, as it expresses itself on the human level, is not less than the evolution of desire.

The awakened human being, whom we often refer to as *Homo amor*, represents a unique and stunning leap in the evolution of desire. At the level of the self-reflective human, we have the capacity to evolve Reality at an entirely new level of clarified desire, which in effect is a new level of consciousness.

- We do this by first becoming conscious of the fact that our lives are characterized by plotlines.
- We become conscious of the vectors of the plotlines of our lives.
- Then we recognize that we can only fully access the unique plotlines of our lives by accessing the unique contours and textures of our unique codes of desire.

Our unique codes of desire are evolution becoming uniquely conscious through each of us.

Moreover, our desire is not static. Our desire is ever evolving because it is ever deepening through a continuous process of clarification.

As self-reflective humans, we can consciously evolve our codes of desire. Our desire is no longer unconscious instinct but conscious choice.

1. The allurement of Reality, the desire of evolution, awakens in us.
2. We then deploy our capacity to clarify our desire. We move from our surface desire to our deepest heart's desire.
3. Our deepest heart's desire is the desire of evolution itself, awake and alive in us, as us, and through us.
4. But our deepest heart's desire is not our generic desire. Rather it is our *unique* desire. It is our unique desire for the unique incarnation of value and Eros—*Eros Value*—that can be lived and loved in us, as us, and through us, unlike anyone else who ever was, is, or will be.
5. Our clarified desire—our deepest heart's desire—participates in the larger Field of Desire.
6. Desire discloses value. Clarified desire discloses clarified

value. Eros is Value, and Value is Eros. There is no split between them. Indeed, they are of a piece and of a word. One word: *ErosValue*.

7. Self-reflective human beings are potentiated to evolve the Field of Desire, and consequently the Field of ErosValue, to an entirely new level or quality of emergence.

8. We do this by clarifying our deepest heart's desire, which is the unique desire of the whole, awake and alive *in me, as me, and through me*.

9. Moreover, desire is not only personal. It is also collective and communal. We are not only individual, self-reflective humans; collectively, we are self-reflective humanity. As such, we are capacitated with some level of choice. We choose to either evolve or devolve as a species.

10. We evolve by clarifying our codes of desire. We devolve by distorting them.

11. When our codes of desire are distorted, we are no longer able to access the self-evident validity of our unique ErosValue. When this happens, we feel fundamentally devalued. This is because—again—Eros is Value, and Value is Eros. When we are de-valued, alienated from our unique participation in the Field of ErosValue, we feel deadened. For Eros is the quality of radical aliveness. To be alienated from Eros is to be deadened.

THE ONLY EFFECTIVE RESPONSE TO THE COLLAPSE OF VALUE IS ITS EVOLUTIONARY RECLAMATION

At the core of the contemporary meta-crisis[1] is the collapse of value. The contemporary *zeitgeist* is postmodern and reductive materialist at its core.

---

1 This term refers to the cascading and interrelated crises across all major sectors of civilization at this complex and climactic moment on the stage of history. We view the meta-crisis as a crisis of maturation—humanity either becomes radically responsible and devoted

As such, inherent value as the ground of Cosmos has been dogmatically disqualified. Indeed, Lewis Mumford called this the "disqualification of the universe."

The only effective and coherent response to the collapse of value is its evolutionary reclamation.

- We recognize that value is a quality of the Real, and that intrinsic value is evolving even as it is eternal.
- We reclaim value by recognizing the dignity and divinity of our desire. Clarified desire discloses value.
- We recognize that desire is not extraneous. Reality *is* desire, and that desire is always desire for ever *greater value*. Reality has *appetition*—in Whitehead's words—for value.
- We reclaim value by recognizing that we participate directly

to life, or this is the end of the human experience. The planetary situation is not some big mistake, or the result of human evil or unredeemable vice. Civilization has been en route to planetary-scale transformation since the first plow, and for millennia the resources of the Earth have been consumed at exponential rates. These next few generations will live during the time when a phase transition to a new level of maturity must occur—that is, wisdom about value commensurate with our technological power must emerge into the heart of culture—or self-induced extinction should be understood as imminent.

Industrialized means of extraction and pollution have reached a planetary scale and are now pushing the very limits of global ecological boundaries, disregulating the biosphere as a whole. As much scientific research has demonstrated, this will quite possibly lead, within a generation or so, to the crossing of multiple tipping points, resulting in an unstoppable degradation and simplification of all Earth systems, as the biosphere cascades into a self-re-enforcing death spiral: dead oceans, desertification, the ending of seasonal rhythms, and a catastrophic depletion of biodiversity. This is the death of Gaia—the end of the biological life support system of Earth—and if humans continue to survive, it will be in conditions of unimaginable extremity.

Indeed, as if in preparation for this, a small number of humans have begun perfecting the instruments and methods of large-scale social control, approaching the limits of human nature, and undermining the basis of modern notions of choice, agency, and self. Digital technologies have accelerated, and there are efforts long underway to transcend politics by way of predictive sciences of human behavioral manipulation. As discussed in the concluding section of this manuscript, we see this as the emergence of planetary-scale TechnoFeudalism. Technologies clustering around the rollout of AI social control are an existential risk—not only because they will kill us all, but because they also have the potential to trap us in subhuman forms of life, as discussed in the book as "the death of *our* humanity."

in the Field of Desire, and that our clarified desire discloses Reality's value that lives both in us and in the Cosmos.

- Reality is animated by desire, so I can trust my desire, and my desire tells me truth. I can trust my body. From Chapter 19 of the Book of Job, as it's read by the interior sciences, says: *Through my body, I vision God*, meaning, *I can trust my body.* **The stirrings of desire in my body**—not in their pseudo-erotic form, not in their addictive form, not in their broken form, but in the form of my *clarified* desire—**discloses value.**
    - It is my desire for creativity.
    - It is my desire for caring.
    - It is my desire for nurturing.
    - It is my desire for responsibility.
    - It is my desire for aliveness.
    - It is my desire for union.
    - It is my desire for ever deeper intimacies, for ever deeper truth-telling, for ever deeper transformation, for ever deeper uniqueness.
- **We realize that through our participation in the Field of Value we are personally implicated in and as evolution**. We not only live in Cosmos, but rather Cosmos lives in us and evolves in us. We participate in the Field of Value and therefore can access it. As such, value is rooted in the eternal yet evolving Field of Value which we access, articulate, clarify, and evolve anthro-ontologically (*anthro* means personhood, which holds in its depth the *ontological*, or real). *I clarify through my own experience what is real.*
- We have the capacity to listen deeply and clarify our interior to listen to the voice of value to which we have direct access. It is value that both evolves through us and at the same time, we bow before it. We bow before the Mystery. We encounter the Mystery, and the Mystery incarnates as value, as Goodness, as

Truth, as Beauty, as the Field of Ethos and Eros, which is one.

- We are participatory with the Infinite in the evolution of ErosValue, which is the evolution of love. We are partners with the infinite Field of Desire. We are partners with the Goddess. We are partners with She. She lives in us, as us, and through us, and we participate in She at the same time.

- We take the baton of the past, and we stand with every human being and with all of life in the present, and we hear the call of the unborn of the future. We are in revolution, and we are in *evolution*. We are evolution in person.

- Desire rages in us—*clarified desire*. That's who we are. We are clarified desire. We are the dawn of the new desire.

- We are at a moment of meta-crisis. There is a decision we have to make about the dignity and divinity of desire. It's a decision about *being* the dawn of desire: as you, as me, as She, as we.

- Our response to the meta-crisis is the Dawn of Desire, in which every human being knows:
  - I am an irreducibly unique incarnation of desire, needed by All-That-Is.
  - I can trust my desire, and my desire tells me truth. I can trust my body.
  - I participate in the Field of Value, and therefore I can clarify value by clarifying my own interior.
  - What I desire becomes the unique value of my life, awake and alive in me.
  - I am a unique incarnation of evolutionary desire. My desire is the desire of Cosmos. It is the telos of Reality itself, living both in me personally and in us collectively.

These oral essays are edited talks delivered by Marc Gafni between November 2022 and March 2024.

CHAPTER ONE

THE HOMO AMOR PRACTICE OF WRITING YOUR OWN SONG OF SONGS—OUTRAGEOUS LOVE LETTERS

Episode 375 (special broadcast) — December 17, 2023

REALITY *IS* CODES OF DESIRE

Reality is codes of desire. That's what Reality is. Reality's not empty, Reality's not hollow. We're not—as T.S. Eliot wrote—*the hollow men and the stuffed men*—we're full. And we're filled with desire. And we're filled with our unique configuration of desire. But that's what Reality is.

Desire is not an aberration; desire is the nature of Cosmos.

The sexual models Eros in that the sexual is defined by, expressed by, and suffused with desire. Sex models Eros, as we've said many times—the entire book *A Return to Eros* is about that topic.

And Eros is the larger Field of Desire which is the field of creative emergence, Reality's desire to generate ever deeper forms of the Good, the True, and the Beautiful, ever deeper forms of value.

Reality at its very core is a story.

It's a love story. But it's not just a love story. It's a Story of LoveDesire.

THE SACRED IS VALUE EXPONENTIALIZED

Our colleague Iain McGilchrist—who just did a dialogue with Zak and offered a beautiful blurb on our new book, *First Principles and First Values*—writing from an entirely different set of sources than I write from, has a sense that there's not just value, but that there's both value and the sacred. This is a distinction I've made for the last thirty years. And the sacred overlaps with value, but it's like value exponentialized—it's the ultimate good; it's the Holy.

The Holy evokes a kind of awestruck rapture, devotion. *"I'm in mad devotion to the Holy, my heart and mind are blown open by the Holy."* It's like the difference between joy and ecstasy: joy is value, and ecstasy is the Holy. It's a blowing open of joy into ecstasy. That's what the holy is. The Holy is the blowing up of value into this ultimate exponential intimacy and goodness.

I recently did a deep dive, from 2am to 5am, an in-depth review of around 200 texts from the classical canon, beginning with Genesis and ending with the end of the prophetic canon, checking the term "sacred" in the sacred texts of the lineage of Solomon. And the term "sacred" in the sacred texts of the lineage of Solomon actually is very close to the word "ultimate intimacy." **The sacred means ultimately intimate.**

ALL THE GREAT TRADITIONS UNDERSTOOD: REALITY *IS* CODES OF DESIRE

The wisdom of Solomon has a primary text. And the primary text of the wisdom of Solomon is the Song of Solomon. The lineage of Solomon writes "All of the books of the sacred texts are sacred, but the ultimate sacred is Holy of Holies." And what's Holy of Holies? The Song of Songs.

This Song of Solomon is the Holy of Holies, the Holy of Holies, it's the Inside of the Inside. And what's it about? It's about desire. It's a song about desire. *Yishakeini mi-neshikot pihu*, "Kiss me with the kisses of your mouth,"

ki-tovim dodecha mi'yayin, "for your Eros, your desire is better than wine."
That's the feeling of the text.

And you can Google a good translation of the text, there's not that many.
We try to do a good translation in Chapter 9 of *A Return to Eros*, but just so
you can feel a couple of the verses: it opens with kissing:

SONG OF SOLOMON

Let him kiss me with the kisses of his mouth, for thy love is better than wine.

His mouth is most sweet, the roof of her mouth is like the best of wine.

Kiss me, all over, all of me. Your lips cover me with kisses.

I have compared thee, oh my love, to a stallion harnessed to one of the great chariots.

While the king was on my couch, my perfume gave forth its fragrance (the fragrance of my tumescence allures the air).

I would cause thee to drink of spiced wine of the juices of my pomegranate.

His left hand is under my head. His right hand embraces me.

Hinach yafeh rayati, how beautiful you are, my beloved.

Your stature is like a palm tree. Your breasts are like its clusters. I say I will climb the palm tree and lay hold to its fruit. Oh, may your breasts be like clusters of the vine and the scent of your breath like apples and your mouth like the best wine.

I am my beloved's, and his desire is for me.

You understand the sense of the text? This is a text which is a code of desire.
And in this text, there's a description of Reality, and Reality is described as
Tocho Ratzuf Ahava, its insides are lined with love, which means that all of
Reality is codes of desire. This notion of Reality being scripts of desire, of
Eros, is the realization of both the interior and exterior sciences. It's what

systems theory and chaos theory and complexity theory are saying. It's what mathematics is pointing towards.

In essence, Reality is coded with patterns of intimacy. Reality is coded with patterns of relationship. That's the nature of Reality. In the great traditions you have always had schools that realize this. They stepped away from the exoteric public teachings of ritual and they said, "No, no, no, actually, the whole thing is codes of desire."

ALWAYS KISSING

They are always kissing, they can't
control themselves.

It is not possible
that any creature can have greater instincts
and perceptions than the
mature human mind.

God ripened me.

So I see it is true:
all objects in existence are
wildly in
love.

Right? That's the realization. The realization, says Meister Eckhart, is that all objects in existence are wildly in love. Writes Meister Eckhart: *Existence leans its mouth towards me, because my love cares for it.* So, in other words, you get this sense. And it lives across traditions. I'll just give you another example, from Saint Thomas Aquinas:

EVERY FOOT A SHRINE

Every creature has a religion.

Every foot is a shrine where
a secret candle burns.
Every cell in us worships
God.

Every arrow in the bow of desire
  has rushed out in hope
  of nearing Him.

Right? And you can find versions of this literally in every single great tradition. I mean, that's essentially what Sufis are talking about. Saint Teresa of Ávila, living at the same time as John of the Cross, writes:

GOD DESIRED ME, SO I CAME CLOSE

God desired me, so I came close.
No one can near God unless
He has prepared a bed for you.
A thousand souls hear His call every second,
  but most everyone then looks into their
  life's mirror and says,
"I am not worthy to leave this sadness."
When I first heard His courting song, I too
  looked at all I had done in my life and said,
"How can I gaze into His omnipresent eyes?"
I spoke those words with all my heart,
  but then He sang again, a song even sweeter,
  and when I tried to shame myself once more
  from His presence
God showed me His compassion and spoke
  a divine truth,
"I made you, Beloved, and all I make is perfect.
Please come close, for I desire you."

In other words, this strain of texts understands that all of Reality is in some fundamental sense this radical Eros, this radical love. It's one of my favorite poems. Another one from Saint Thomas Aquinas:

HIS CHOIR

Sing, my tongue; sing, my hand;
  sing, my feet; my knee,
  my loins, my

whole body.
Indeed I am His
  choir.

Hafiz writes:

LIKE PASSIONATE LIPS

There are
So many positions of
Love:
Each curve on a branch,
The thousand different ways
Your eyes can embrace us,
The infinite shapes your
Mind can draw,
The spring
Orchestra of scents,
The currents of light combusting
Like passionate lips,
The revolution of Existence's skirt
Whose folds contain other worlds,
Your every sigh that falls against
His inconceivable
Omnipresent
Body.

Hafiz:

If God
Invited you to a party
And said,

'Everyone
In the ballroom tonight
Will be my special
Guest...'

How would you then treat them
When you

Arrived?

Indeed, indeed!

And I know
There is no one in this world

Who
Is not upon
His Jeweled Dance
Floor

—and Hafiz knows that there is no one in this world who is not standing on Her jeweled dance floor.

Again, Hafiz:

I HAVE COME INTO THIS WORLD TO SEE THIS

I have come into this world to see this:
    the sword drop from men's hands even at the height
    of their arc of anger
    because we have finally realized there is just one flesh to wound
    and it is His—the Christ's, our Beloved's.

I have come into this world to see this: all creatures hold hands as
    we pass through this miraculous existence we share on the way
    to even a greater being of soul,
    a being of just ecstatic light, forever entwined and at play
    with Him.

I have come into this world to hear this:
    every song the earth has sung since it was conceived in
    the Divine's womb and began spinning from
    His wish,

Every song by wing and fin and hoof,
Every song by hill and field and tree and woman and child,
Every song of stream and rock,
Every song of tool and lyre and flute,
Every song of gold and emerald and fire,
Every song the heart should cry with magnificent dignity

to know itself as God:
for all other knowledge will leave us again in want and aching –
only imbibing the glorious Sun
will complete us.

I have come into this world to experience this:
men so true to love
they would rather die before speaking
an unkind
word,
men so true their lives are His covenant—
the promise of hope.

I have come into this world to see this:
the sword drop from men's hands
even at the height of
their arc of
rage
because we have finally realized
there is just one flesh
we can wound.

Indeed, we have finally realized that there's just one flesh to wound, and it is His, the Christ's, our beloved's. He writes:

Know
The true nature of your Beloved.
In His loving eyes your every thought,
Word and movement is always—
Always Beautiful.

And:

One regret, dear world,
That I am determined not to have
When I am lying on my deathbed
Is that
I did not kiss you enough

And then finally—this is about a courtesan:

Quietly her fame spread,
  the courtesan who few had heard of a year ago.
Shy men could do with her what they could do with no one else,
  and women too sought her breasts
  and came to know how wonderful touch could be.
And she wrote poems and left her eyes there
  for they were what loved the most.

Here's the last stanza again: *And she wrote poems and left her eyes there—* meaning she left her eyes in the poem, *for they—*her eyes—*were what loved the most.* And so, this sense of "she wrote poems," this writing of poems, these are all forms of the Song of Songs. These are forms of *Shir HaShirim.* These are forms of the Song of Solomon. And we've given a name to this in CosmoErotic Humanism.

We've called these poems Outrageous Love Letters. In other words, what we've basically said is, in this new Story of Value called CosmoErotic Humanism: **We have to democratize great love.**

You begin to see that's what *Homo amor* is.[1] ***Homo amor* is the democratization of great love in which**—I don't leave it to Rumi, I don't leave it to Hafiz, I don't leave it to Rabia, I don't leave it to Saint John of the Cross, I don't leave it to Teresa of Ávila—**I *become* Outrageous Love.**

And by Outrageous Love, we mean something very precise. By Outrageous Love we mean not love as a social construction, but that Reality is a love story, all the way up and all the way down. *I'm a unique script of desire*

---

1 *Homo amor* is the emergence of the new human and the new humanity.
This new human understands that she is a unique configuration of value; that the core value of Cosmos is intimacy—Eros—expressed as irreducible uniqueness, in ever deeper levels of communion.
  · *Homo amor* understands that she is the CosmoErotic Universe in person.
  · *Homo amor* understands that she is the Amorous Cosmos in person.
  · *Homo amor* understands that she is the evolutionary impulse in person; the impulse of Evolutionary Love beats uniquely in her heart.
Or said in the classical language of the great traditions: *Homo amor* understands that she is the language of God: she is God's verb, noun, adjective and dangling modifier. She is God's eyes. The ways she loves God is to let God see through her eyes. The way she loves Reality— herself, humanity, all living beings—she loves by seeing *through* God's eyes.

in that Reality, and I have the capacity to be a mad lover. We're trying to come together and form this intimate communion which then forms this revolution to tell this new Story of Value, which is what happened in Florence in the Renaissance. We have to come together as Outrageous Lovers. We have to come together as a *Chevreya Kadisha*, a band of the sacred—but the sacred means ultimate intimacy.

THE SACRED MEANS ULTIMATE INTIMACY

And I mean that philologically. Philologically, the sacred means ultimate intimacy. There's a man named Eliezer Berkovits, who when he died, his son gave me the key to his apartment, and I went through all his books. And he had a book that he had published in Wayne State University Press which is a book where he did a philological examination of the term, "the sacred." And I came to the same conclusion that he did, and I was ecstatic to read him, and I don't know if this essay is actually republished anywhere, but he actually understood—that the sacred means ultimate intimacy. That's what the sacred means.

The intimate and the sacred are the same.

THE DEMOCRATIZATION OF FLAMING GREAT LOVE

The Song of Songs is Holy of Holies, means it's the intimate of intimate. Meaning, it's a love story. But if I democratize enlightenment, I've got to democratize great love. And in a book called *Radical Kabbalah*, I was privileged many years ago to talk about the democratization of enlightenment. Democratization of enlightenment means that all of us should have an experience of True Self, where *I experience myself as part of the enlightened field. I'm not separate from the field.* That's the first step. And in *Unique Self*, we talked about the democratization of enlightenment. But now we need to go the next step.

And the next step is the democratization of flaming great love. We need to literally become Outrageous Lovers. We need to become evolutionary lovers and say, *I am great love.* And *I am great love* means *I don't leave it to Rumi.* We often say that when we want to send someone a love note, we send them some words written by a dead Persian—with all due respect to Persians. Not a good idea.

I am Rumi, I am Solomon, I am Meister Eckhart. Most of us have written love poems at one point in our lives. At some point *I wrote a couple of words in a love poem*, and then we stop, because they're a little stilted and they're a little convoluted and they take a little time and they make us feel a little funny. But remember *that little moment where I wrote to some beloved of mine*—it might have been my child, it might have been a partner, it might have been a friend—*I wrote them a little stilted love note, and then I kind of quit and I sent people Rumi poems.* Don't do that.

Write Outrageous Love Letters. The idea of writing Outrageous Love Letters is the practice of the Song of Songs.

The Song of Songs is *literally* a series of Outrageous Love notes between a lover and a beloved. That's what it is. And if you all follow the exegesis on the Song of Songs and you read the Song of Songs, carefully, you realize these are love notes between a lover and a beloved. So, there's a whole strain in scholarship which says, *this book is not sacred—it's just a bunch of tavern songs, mere love notes.* And sometimes, scholarship can be excessive in its idiocy.

Of course they're tavern songs. That's the point. The point is, *that's what they know in the tavern.* What they understand in the tavern is that:

It's all a love song.

11

My life is destitute and I'm wrecked and I'm poor.
But oh my God in the love song, it all stops for a moment, and it's
good. I can feel the gorgeous delightful pleasure of Reality, alive
and awake and enflaming, and I don't wait for someone else to
do it.

I don't want to read Rumi,
I want to be Rumi.

I don't want to *read* the Song of Songs—although it's a great idea—I want to *be* the Song of Songs. But I can't just be the Song of Songs. I've got to be love in action. I am evolutionary desire. I'm evolutionary love desire. And evolution is love in action that lives uniquely in me, which is my unique script of desire, yes, and yes, and yes.

But there's a practice, just like there was a practice of prayer, there's a practice of study called the "Intellectual Amorous"—the intellectual embrace of the Divine, which Chaim of Volozhin talks about in a book called *Nefesh ha-Chayim, The Soul of Life* in section four. It's a stunning book.

So, there's an intellectual embrace of Divine, there's praxis, there's prayer, there's study, there's meditation. In classical meditation, *I try to access and locate myself in the Field of True Self, the Field of Awareness,* but there's a new practice. And the new practice is the new practice of *Homo amor.* **The new practice is the practice of writing Outrageous Love Letters.**

Now, when I write an Outrageous Love Letter, how do I do it? Let's get real for a second, okay? Let's get real.

THE *HOMO AMOR* PRACTICE OF WRITING OUTRAGEOUS LOVE LETTERS

The way you write an Outrageous Love letter is you have to first bracket your ego, because your ego is hearing what you write and it wants to remain socially acceptable and proper and appropriate and even though you're writing it yourself, you're afraid that somebody is going to read it someplace, some imaginary person in your early life is going to read this and you're like, *Oh my God, I can't have somebody read this, maybe it's going to be discovered.* But it's not a real worry, it's like this inner voice. You have to bracket the voice of the ego. You have to actually access the fullness of the field running through you.

Then what you have to do is *you've got to wildly exaggerate until you're accurate.* That's how you become accurate.

When you wildly exaggerate, you become accurate. That's an Outrageous Love Letter.

And then you've got to write Outrageous Love Letters every day. *It's got to be part of my fabric, just like I breathe, I write Outrageous Love Letters. I can write them to myself, I can write them to a friend, I can write them to a beloved, I can write them to a cab driver that I met.* In other words, writing Outrageous Love Letters is the democratization of great love. *I'm a great lover, I'm a unique script of LoveDesire and I'm writing Outrageous Love Letters.*

Outrageous Love Letters are the new Song of Songs. We're literally writing sacred texts. They're the new Song of Songs.

Now, there are two forms of Outrageous Love Letters. So, the funny thing to say here would be, *make sure there's no kids around*, but that's actually not right. It's a point that Warren Farrell has made in his writing and we've all noticed it, but I want to credit Warren because he wrote about it thirty years ago, which is when parents walk through and they see their kids watching TV and they're seeing their kids watching this excessively violent film—people are killing each other, smashing each other—they walk by, *ah, kids are occupied, good, it's all good*, but if you walk through and, I mean, God forbid, there's some breast showing, *oh my God, what are you watching? It's terrible.*

You have to understand that that actually goes into the child. It's actually a traumatization. I'm not saying that you should have displays of private intimacies on public networks. My point is the trauma that we feel around it. That's a different conversation. But the trauma we feel around it actually pours into the child. It feels like *something's wrong here.* There's something wrong.

MARY'S MOSAIC

There's a book which is on my bookshelf someplace called *Mary's Mosaic*, it's an incredible book. *Mary's Mosaic* is about a woman who had an affair with J.F.K., and she was killed several months after he was killed. The Central Intelligence Agency, Northern Virginia, Washington scene—they were the masters of the universe.

This is not conspiracy theory, there's an enormous amount of documentation that whatever happened with John F. Kennedy's assassination certainly wasn't a lone gunman. That's for sure. There's an enormous amount of information on that. That's not our topic.

And so very early on, Mary, who had this significant affair with Kennedy, starts saying, "They killed him." Her husband was one of the senior guys at the CIA—it's a long story. She was killed jogging six or eight months later, however that happened. And, a friend of her son's writes this book about her, called Mary's Mosaic, and it's a book about that era and that story, and it's kind of an unknown book. It's quite good. You want to capture something of America of that era, something of Eros, it's a fascinating book. And there's one scene where this friend of her son's writes that he came to their house—she's the wife of a major CIA executive, if you will, so they're living in a sprawling Washington or Virginia home—and he comes over and his friend doesn't realize he's coming over. So, he comes to the backyard, and he sees her bathing naked in the backyard.

And he tells this beautiful story where *she sees him, he sees her, and she looks up at him, and she just smiles, this gentle, profound, beautiful purity, smile.* She didn't go like, *Aaah!* She just smiled, like the Goddess smiled, and just nodded. And the kid says, he nodded. And he respectfully turned around and went the other way. **And he said, in that moment, he knew what purity meant, he knew what Goodness meant.**

Can you feel that? It's like, wow. Right? That's the Goddess. That's the Goddess. She knows the truth. There's always the Goddess. And sometimes the Goddess is the mother, and sometimes the Goddess is the courtesan as we just read in Hafiz, and sometimes the Goddess is the sister, sometimes the Goddess is the beloved.

So, that's this notion of Outrageous Love Letters.

And then there's Outrageous Erotic Love Letters. And Outrageous Erotic Love Letters are the same as Outrageous Love Letters, but they translate into Eros. To write an Outrageous Erotic Love Letter is to write to a beloved of their dazzling beauty. What is the Song of Solomon? It's not an Outrageous Love Letter, it's an Outrageous Erotic Love Letter.

And I always say somewhat jokingly that *you write Outrageous Love Letters to young, old, men, women, all fluid genders in between, and small mammals,* just to kind of cover everything. But the point is Outrageous Love Letters, it's the structure of Reality.

We've exiled love, we've made it so narrow and so small.

- ◆ Reality is codes of desire.
- ◆ The Song of Songs is an expression of Reality's code of desire.
- ◆ The democratization of the Song of Songs is: *I become Solomon, I become Rumi.* And when *I become Rumi* and *I become Solomon*, I write Outrageous Love Letters because

15

what the Song of Songs is, it's Outrageous Love Letters.

And so, by the way, just to say, my detractors—of which there are a number in the world, I haven't met most of them, probably 99% don't bother meeting or talking to me, but my detractors—the way they would tell the story is, "Oh, my, this is just an excuse to be sexual," which is, of course, ridiculous.

First off, *it demonizes sexuality, as if it was bad.* That's problem one.

But problem two is *that's not the point; the whole thing's about Eros.*

When you don't have an experience of God, and you're a scholar for example, you say that God is a construct created as a human crutch because you have no experience of it. So, what must it be? That's the only thing it could be.

If you have no experience of Outrageous Love, the only way you could interpret someone writing Outrageous Love Letters is: "It must be some sort of fiendish maneuver for some sort of totalitarian control of some kind of sinister kind"—because you've never experienced it in your body, in your heart, in your soul. **There's nothing more awake and more alive than writing an Outrageous Erotic Love Letter, or an Outrageous Love Letter.**

When you're writing an Outrageous Love Letter, you don't say to yourself, "What's the meaning of existence? I wonder. Huh, not sure." Right? So, we write each other, men and men, women and women. And there are different moments, it evolves.

There's one beautiful couple who went out for a while in the Center, and they stopped going out, and he said to she in this particular case, "For the six months after we're not going out anymore, I want to write you Outrageous Love Letters." What a beautiful thing to do, right?

In other words, instead of love being this egoic structure, where "If we're not going out in that formal way, we've got to change the locks and demonize each other"—no, no, "We were together for a period of time and it was very beautiful, and now, in our separation, we're going to love each other in a new way. We're going to write Outrageous Love Letters."

It would be a different world if people separated and for six months wrote each other Outrageous Love Letters as part of the separation. We'd be living in a different universe.

That's Outrageous Love.

That's this notion of codes of desire.

CHAPTER TWO

REWRITING THE SCRIPT OF DESIRE: FOR WOMEN, FOR LIFE, FOR FREEDOM—MAHSA AMINI DID NOT DIE IN VAIN

Episode 318 — November 13, 2022

AT THIS PRECISE MOMENT, JUST LIKE DYSTOPIA HOVERS, SO DOES UTOPIA

We're meeting each other in this moment of revolution. I want to welcome everyone to this place.

Who are we? We are the revolution itself.

And what is the revolution? The revolution is the experience, the knowing, that we are at this moment of meta-crisis, and we have the capacity in this moment of meta-crisis to be something *more*, to be something *deeper*, to realize the deeper dimensions of our joy and the deeper dimensions of our power.

In this moment of meta-crisis, we are quite literally poised between dystopia and utopia. We have this very real dystopian possibility of extinction—the dystopian possibility of collapse of world systems (in a kind of *Mad Max* way, if you remember that movie), a dystopian stagnation in which the world turns into a caste system, which makes India look like Athenian democracy at its best.

Think *Hunger Games*—if you want to use a cinematic reference—in which a tiny elite rules the rest of society, and where freewill and human choice and human self-creation and our inward spaces of meaning are crushed by a totalitarian order, which imposes its will through artificial intelligence, and which dominates in the planetary stack in every dimension of our being (because we have to have our identity number in the system to survive). And the emotional sensors of "affective computing," which is also called "Emotional AI," literally read our every emotion. And if we don't align with the larger system, we're thrown off the system and we die. And within two generations, the very quality of our humanity has been killed.

We're in this moment where we're poised between dystopia and utopia.

We must invest that same world infrastructure with a new superstructure—borrowing that term from Marvin Harris, the sociologist and historian; by superstructure we mean a new Story of Value, rooted in First Principles and First Values.

We are at this moment of meta-crisis in which we're threatened by exponential technology which animates a global civilization.

We are at this moment in which every civilization has crashed and we haven't solved the self-terminating structures that have crashed those civilizations. And now the civilization is global, with exponential technology.

And yet, **at this precise moment, just like dystopia hovers, so does utopia.** There's a utopian possibly. And by utopian, I don't mean *la-di-da*, I don't mean fanciful, I don't mean fairy tale—I mean the beginning of a true utopia, of utopia grounded in Reality, which is the most beautiful world that we know deep inside of us is possible. And we can imagine that world, and we *know* that world. And we know that utopia also beckons at the door. And for that utopia to happen, we need to change not just the infrastructure, we need to change the superstructure. **We need to be the storytellers of Reality, and to realize that we are the new chapter in that story, and to know that that story is a Story of Value.** That's r/evolution, friends.

CREATING THE FUTURE AS *HOMO AMOR*

Today we're going to do something very special. I'm trembling a little bit because of the honor that we need to give to She—to Eros herself, to what the interior sciences called the Goddess, what David Bohm (the physicist student of Einstein) called the Implicate Order; what others have simply called Infinite Reality.

We need to honor Reality today.

And particularly, we need to turn to Reality, to turn to a particular dimension of the meta-crisis, and we need to honor it and understand it in an entirely new way, to actually get beneath the headlines, and to understand what are the failed superstructures, the failed stories of value that are generating the action.

Today, we're going to be talking about Mahsa Amini.

Mahsa Amini, who gave her life as She. We're going to be talking about what underlies the murder of Eros, which was the murder of Mahsa Amini in Iran. And we're going to be talking about how we actually honor Mahsa Amini as She and understand, in a profound and radical way, what's actually happening here.

We shine the light of First Values and First Principles, of this new Story of Value, what we call CosmoErotic Humanism, on this moment, to participate directly in the evolution of the source code; the evolution of consciousness in culture.

Oh my God, I'm trembling, madly joyous for the privilege of us being together today in this moment, and in this place, and in this time. So thank you, everyone, for being here. And let's see if we can just drop in and find our way. And we're here not to be entertained, we're not going to do wisdo-tainment.

We are here because we are the Unique Self Symphony. We are the band of Evolutionary Lovers. We are da Vinci. Imagine the Renaissance, the

Renaissance which is the time between worlds and this time between stories. And we're in a similar moment. We're in a moment of what we called a few weeks ago, neuro-cultural-plasticity. We're in a moment in which it could all change. There's not yet a values lock-in. We have the capacity to create the future. And we *need* to create the future.

We need to create the future as *Homo amor*. *Homo amor* is the new human and the new humanity that emerges as the primary response to the meta-crisis. The primary qualities of *Homo amor*, the fulfillment of *Homo sapiens*, are:

1. *Homo amor* embodies in her very being a universal grammar of value as a context for our diversity. *Homo amor is* value; *Homo amor* is value incarnate. And *Homo amor* speaks this new language, this new universal grammar of value, which is a context for our diversity.

2. *Homo amor* is intimate. *Homo amor* is intimate with the past. *Homo amor* is intimate with the depth of the present. But *Homo amor* is also intimate with the future. And we can feel the cry and the call of the unborn, even as we feel the call of every human being on the face of the planet now, including the 2 billion who don't have access to clean water on a regular basis. And we feel the demand of the past that turns to us and passes us the baton, and says, *all of our unfinished business depends on you.*

And so we're trembling, but we're trembling with joy, with a kind of ecstatic urgency at the privilege of stepping in in this moment in history. So we're going to enter today, as best as She allows us.

And I'm sure we'll make mistakes, but **we're going to make mistakes—with Her grace—in the right direction.**

We're going to enter into the honor, the dignity of Mahsa Amini.

EVOLUTIONARY LOVE CODE: RADICAL ALIVENESS IS LIFE

Radical aliveness is life.

We yearn for life.

But when we are deadened, we move to kill life as a shortcut to genuine aliveness.

The murder of Eros is sourced in the failure of Eros.

We cannot become *Homo amor* until we transcend the impulse to murder Eros.

To transcend the impulse we must first fearlessly recognize it.

Reality is Eros. Reality is She. Reality is He and She in all gendered forms. Reality is She and He, uniquely, Krishna and Radha—in all of Her sacred wild expressions.

We're here to evolve the source code, so here we go. And thank you everyone for the depth of your presence in this Unique Self Symphony. So here we go, friends.

Oh my God—total joy, total heartbreak, but total heart open, total beauty.

MAHSA AMINI SACRIFICED HER LIFE FOR EROS

I'm going read a text that we just wrote spontaneously yesterday morning. And I want to just slowly and gently read that text for you, and we're going to begin from there.

> *Did Mahsa Amini die in vain? Mahsa Amini was killed on September 17, 2022. And Mahsa Amini was the Goddess; Mahsa Amini was Eros. And her murder was the murder of the Goddess; her murder was the murder of Eros.*

She was arrested, my friends, for wearing her hijab—the Islamic head-covering mandated by Ayatollah Khomeini when he took power in Iran—

for wearing it "improperly," and for her pants being slightly too tight. Mahsa Amini was not an activist; she was not involved—as her brother reports—in the political struggles of Iran. She lived in a small village. She was modest, shy, inordinately good.

She had gone to Tehran to visit her brother and was arrested while with her family. Placed in a van, she was beaten by the police because she refused to accommodate, to bend, to be degraded by their insults. Because somehow, she knew in that moment, that their offense to her offended She, offended Reality, offended Eros itself. She understood that their insult insulted *value* itself. That it insulted the Good, the True, and the Beautiful.

And in that moment—according to the eyewitnesses that were in the van with her—she could have submitted, she could have bowed, she could have allowed the degradation and lived. But **she somehow, intuitively, magically, mystically understood—in a way that defies expression in words—that to allow the insult to her being in that moment was a violation of life itself.** And so Mahsa Amini paid the ultimate price. She sacrificed her life for She, as She. **She sacrificed her life for Eros.** She sacrificed her life—and we're going to unpack this today, for us.

Her death has rightly sparked explosions of sacred protest, all through Iran and around the world; explosions of value, explosions of Eros, explosions of human Goodness, Truth, and Beauty. And the protesters are coming from all walks of Iranian society, and all walks in every socioeconomic and cultural level from around the world. The protesters have been killed, beaten and tortured, hundreds, men and women, again and again and again.

And at this moment, friends, we're gathering today. And we're gathering to honor the Goddess and to answer one question: **Did Mahsa Amini die in vain?** And the answer of course is *no, of course not.* But there's only one way to make that knowing true, to answer that question. And that is to—together today—enter into what the lineage calls *umka d'umka* in Aramaic: *the depths of the depths. Lifnai v'lifnim*: to the inside of the inside. To Sanctum Sanctorum, *Kodesh HaKodashim*—in the language of the Aramaic lineage—to the *Holy of Holies*, to the Sanctum Sanctorum of human meaning, of human devotion, of human value, of human Eros. And to understand what's at stake here.

THERE'S NO SPLIT BETWEEN EROS AND ETHICS

What do we mean by the Goddess? It's not a mainstream word that we hear often. But actually, without understanding that word, you actually can't understand physics or biochemistry or molecular biology. *What do we mean when we say She? What is this Eros we're talking about, and what does it mean to murder Eros?* But perhaps, friends, exponentially more importantly—to ensure that this murder of Eros wasn't in vain, that Mahsa Amini didn't die in vain—we have to answer these questions:

- ◆ What does it mean to live in Eros and as Eros?
- ◆ What does it mean that all ethics are rooted in Eros?
- ◆ What does it mean that the clash between the erotic and the ethical that's assumed by all of society is a false clash?

We assume that the erotic and the ethical oppose each other, that we need to curb Eros in order to be ethical. Mahsa Amini's hair, her embodiment is understood to be a threat by the Ayatollahs, somehow "it will undermine ethos." But actually—and we're going to go so deep into this today on so many levels—**the erotic and the ethical don't oppose each other.**

I was privileged in 2003 to write an article called "On the Erotic and the Ethical," featured on the cover of one of the leading intellectual magazines in the United States. There was a great outcry attacking the cover, and the morality police—in their American and Israeli forms—came out; not to kill me physically, but to murder Eros nonetheless.

We're going to unpack this today. I know this is just words now, but we're going to go so deep into what these words mean. First let's get the meta-context together.

In truth there's not only no split between Eros and ethics. Actually, every failure of ethics—every murder, every contraction, every pettiness, every deceit, all acting out, all violation—*all of it is a direct result of the collapse of Eros.*

This is one of the core principles of CosmoErotic Humanism:

All ethical breakdown derives ultimately from the prior breakdown of Eros itself.

The only way, friends, to reclaim ethos—to reclaim goodness, and kindness, and sensitivity, and radical empathy, and open heart, and the sacredness of shared joy and tears, and the delight and wild gratitude for each other, for our eyes, for our hearts, for our souls, for our embodiment, for the wonder of being—is to reclaim and know the wonder of being an embodied incarnate human; a unique incarnation of Eros, fully alive, fully awake, wildly good, and wildly free.

The only way to get home to that place is to reclaim Eros as the nature of Reality and its deepest realization.

To reclaim Eros in its deepest expression means to reclaim Eros in its most profound, urgent, ecstatic meaning as the very source code of Cosmos—of the entire physical universe, of all of the exterior sciences, and all of the interior sciences—*to know that Reality itself is Eros.*

That's what we're going to talk about today:

- We're going to talk about Eros.
- We're going to talk about fundamentalism.
- We're going to talk about pornography.
- We're going to talk about violations of Eros.

We're going to talk about what it means to murder Eros, and how we engage in the evolution of Eros. And we're coming together, all of us from around the world, in **a Unique Self Symphony of Eros.**

And so tenderly, friends, with so much respect and so much honor, I want to invite you—we want to invite each other, as you and me and we—to be here today, **knowing that you're bringing yourself as a unique incarnation of Eros.** That's actually who we are. You are, I am, we are. You are a unique incarnation of divine aliveness.

You're a unique configuration of intimacy, a unique pattern of desire, that never was, is, or will be ever again.

Know that your Eros and your aliveness and your intimacy and your desire is precious before She, is precious before the Divine. But friends, it's not only that your Eros is precious before the Divine. It goes even deeper. In your *unique* Eros—in your intimacy, in your *unique* intimacy, in your desire, in your *unique* configuration of desire, in your aliveness, in your irreducibly unique aliveness—in all of that, **She—Reality—finds Her own self-fulfillment, Her own self-realization.**

Quite literally, based on the best integration of the interior and exterior sciences, we can say this careful sentence in the new Story of Value:

She shudders in self-recognition as She feels the shudder moving through your body, crying out Her name: Oh God.

So we come together, my friends, to know, to cry out, and to scream in pain, and to cry out in great joy, in gratitude on our knees in devotion to She, to Mahsa Amini, and to each and every one of the other men and women who died for us, for we, for She.

And to say to them, **you did not die in vain; your death sparked Eros Herself.**

You aroused the Goddess, and She is here, and She is awake, and She is alive.

BROTHERS, THERE'S ALWAYS A PATH HOME

And finally, friends, one more word to the police in the van who beat Mahsa Amini—but *the police* is also just a tagline; we can't see the faces of those boys.

So to those young men—raised on a deadening, degraded propaganda which was anti-life, raised on a propaganda which didn't understand the Eros of goodness, which didn't understand the value of Eros and Eros of value, which didn't understand the Eros of Beauty and the Eros of Truth— men who felt alienated from themselves, men who viewed their own sexing as a violation of She (because that's what was brainwashed; that's what contaminated their psyche from their earliest memory), men who were brutalized by a teaching that was false and that took the name of Goddess in vain, men who were traumatized by their own experience of their own bodies, men who were shamed, at the very core of their being, and were tormented by the system that created and controlled them.

So to those men, we say:

Brothers, there's always a path home, young men!

There's always a path to liberation.

We're not here to demonize you, we're here to demand your transformation.

There's always a path home.

Find, brothers, the goodness in your own hearts.

Find the kindness in your own hearts.

Find your way to understanding that your embodiment is good.

And that the feelings of Eros that pulse through you, if you trace them back to their roots, they're not in violation of the Prophet; they're not in violation of Islam.

They are the deepest expression of Allahu Akbar, of the great surrender to the goodness which is Goddess. They are the deepest expression of She.

I—we—can't forgive you young men. It's not ours to do. But you have to ask for forgiveness, and it will be granted. You have to find your way home, and you can, and you must, and you will.

That would mean, in an unimaginable way, friends, that Mahsa Amini didn't die in vain.

And to Mahsa Amini's brother and to her father and mother, whose hearts are ripped out—and to the fathers and mothers and brothers and sisters of every protester who has been killed in Iran in these weeks and in previous years—we're in devotion to you; you're our heroes, you're our teachers.

Go in peace to the next stage of your journey. And be with us from the next world if you can right now, as we gather around the world sparked by your spirit, which is the spirit of She; sparked by the flame of Eros and ethics that lit up your heart, that now flames as unimaginable beauty in our world. For that, we come together right now.

BARAYE: TO LIVE FOR THE GREAT EROS OF REALITY

We're going to play a song now called "Baraye," which was written by Shervin Hajipour, and it's become the anthem of this Mahsa Amini revolution. There are three versions of the song, and we're going to come to each of them. The word *Baraye* means *for:* I'm doing this *for*.

Just so everyone understands, these tweets that you see—they're going to kind of show up on the text of the song—these are the tweets that Shervin, who's the songwriter, received; these tweets of protest and outrage. And he turns these tweets into the song. So the tweets will come up as he chants the song. Let's go inside, friends. Oh, my God!

So what's Baraye? *Baraye* means *for*. It's to be intimate with Reality, with her joy and her suffering, and to live *for*: *for* the great Eros of Reality. *Baraye*, in one lineage tradition in the Renaissance, was expressed in the following way:

Leshem yichud: for the sake of the union of the coming together of He and She in all Her gendered forms. Leshem yichud: that everything I do is for that great coming together.

Reality is Eros, moving towards its own evolution; to ever deeper levels of the Good, the True, and the Beautiful.

THE NEW STORY OF DESIRE: REALITY *IS* EROS

What is the new Story of Value, which integrates the deepest validated insights of all the interior sciences and all the exterior sciences—premodern, modern, and postmodern? You could sum it up in three words, which are in today's code.

Reality is Eros.

That's what Reality is. At its very core, the nature of Reality is Eros. We live in what I want to call a CosmoErotic Universe. It's Eros all the way up and all the way down. And we wrote a sacred text, *A Return to Eros*, which tells the story. *A Return to Eros*, which I wrote with Dr. Kristina Kincaid, is about this realization that Reality is Eros. And that Eros drives Reality, it animates Reality.

And what is Eros? Eros is the core pulse of evolution itself, that seeks, that desires—because Reality *desires*—ever deeper contact and ever greater wholeness.

- That Eros animates the four forces of Reality: the strong and the weak nuclear, the electromagnetic, and the gravitational.
- That Eros drives Reality towards ever deeper and newer expressions of value, of Goodness, Truth, and Beauty.
- That Eros is desire, that Eros is animated by desire itself.

It's why Alfred North Whitehead—who wrote *Principia Mathematica* with George Bertrand Russell—talks about *the appetites of Cosmos*. Because Cosmos desires, and desire can't be split off. And Cosmos moves us all the way through the world of matter and the world of life and the world of mind, the self-reflective human mind, through the impulse power of desire: for more laughter, for more value, for more Goodness, for more Truth, for more Beauty.

And that desire awakens in us in an irreducibly unique way, and that's what we call Unique Self. Every human being is a unique incarnation of Eros. Every human being is an irreducibly unique incarnation of desire.

> *Every human being is an irreducibly unique incarnation of desire which is value. Desire itself has value. That's the very nature of Reality.*

What does that have to do with Mahsa Amini? What does that have to do with a hijab? What does that have to do with pants that are too tight?

We need, friends, **a narrative of desire; we need a story of desire. We need a story of sexuality. We need a sexual narrative.**

THE FOUR SEXUAL NARRATIVES IN REALITY TODAY

We have four sexual narratives in Reality today, which we talk about in *A Return to Eros*.

1. The first narrative—which is held by the morality police in Tehran—is **sex-negative**: "Sex violates the Prophet. Sex violates ethos. Sex is somehow the great cosmic violation, and we need to split off the sexual in order to get to the ethical. Sex is dangerous."

Are they right that sex is dangerous? Of course they're right that sex is dangerous. But they go from dangerous to evil, where the physical incarnate embodiment of Eros that lives in we, in she, in thee, in me, is viewed as evil, and only the splitting off of that unique desire allows me to be purified. That's sex-negative. We reject sex-negative, but we haven't responded to that in the rest of the world with anything compelling. We reject sex-negative, but what do we replace it with?

- We replace it with a second narrative of desire or of sex, which is **sex-neutral.** Alfred Charles Kinsey, the sex researcher, is sex-neutral. "Sex is just like having lunch." But that's not true, sex is *not* like having lunch. It's not mere biology.

- We have a third sexual narrative or story of desire that goes through the world, which is **sex-positive.** The sexual revolution, sex-positive. "Sex is a positive social force. It breeds satisfaction and cohesion, and makes you feel better, and have more balance in your life." Well, that's just too bland, that's too weak, that's too insipid. Sex is more than merely positive.

- Then there's the fourth sexual narrative which says, **sex is sacred when you're having a baby.** There's some version of that narrative that appears sometimes in fundamentalism, in many places around the world. But again, it's not quite right, because we live in a moment of population explosion, and ninety-nine percent of sex that happens in the world is *not* to have a baby. How many people here, the last time you had sex, engaged sexually in order to have a baby? I would wager, almost no one. And babies are gorgeous and babies

31

are important and babies are stunning, and I have four of the most beautiful kids in the world. And the moment of their birth and the moment of their creation are a wonder of wonders and miracle of miracles.

- ◆ Sex is not limited in its sacredness to procreation. Sex is not sacred "because it creates life." It's much deeper. **Sex is sacred because it *is* life.**

EROS IS NOT MERE SENTIMENT; IT IS THE HEART OF EXISTENCE ITSELF

Sex is sacred because it *is* life. That's the new story of desire that emerges from this integration of all the great truths in the world.

We call it in CosmoErotic Humanism: sex-erotic. Sex-erotic understands that the desire that rises in me uniquely is rooted in the Field of Desire. Sex-erotic says that:

The Eros that drives Reality from the very inception—from the first Big Bang, from the very explosion of the original singularity, and drives the world of subatomic particles, all of gravity and all of electromagnetism and all of the strong and weak nuclear forces, and which moves through the entire biosphere, the entire world of biology, and which emerges in the depths of the self-reflective human, and drives all the stages of human evolution and transformation—**the Eros that moves the Sun and other stars, as Dante once wrote, is not mere human sentiment; it's the heart of existence itself.**

So when *sexual* desire arises in me—yes, it needs the right context, yes, it needs the right place and the right person, of course—but at the core, **that actual experience of desire *is* the desire of Reality arising in me uniquely.**

And until I know that, I'm shamed.

Until I know that, my experience is of radical shame. And shame means—not that I made a mistake, not that I did something bad.

---

*The experience of shame
is that I am bad, that I'm
broken, that I can't be fixed.*

And that is the experience that arises in the entire leadership of fundamentalisms the world over, which is why fundamentalisms always become cruel in some way. They become cruel because the leaders of fundamentalism are fundamentally shamed in their very experience of their own being, in their very experience of their own desire. Because they don't have a story of desire equal to their experience.

The first response—to promise Mahsa Amini that She, the Goddess, didn't die in vain, that Eros is not murdered, that Eros is evolving and is resurrected—**is to tell, at the very center of the new Story of Value, a new Story of Desire, and of the inherent and intrinsic and wild dignity and divinity of desire.**

Let's go back to our chant for today. Let's go back to *Baraye, for the sake of it.*

For the sake of it all. We can *feel* it. And the depth of this knowing of the interior and exterior sciences, you can express in one sentence: **the Universe feels, and the Universe feels Love; the Universe feels, and the Universe feels Eros.**

And let's see if we can find this. The Universe feels, and the Universe feels uniquely through me, in a way that It doesn't feel through anyone else that ever was, is, or will be. And we can feel each other, and the way we feel each other is through our unique incarnation and shudder of desire. That's how we find each other.

Uniqueness is not separation. Uniqueness is the currency of connection. It's what creates the Unique Self Symphony.

TWO WAYS TO MURDER EROS: THE MORALITY POLICE AND THE SEX-POSITIVE LIBERAL RESPONSE

Let's go one step deeper. Are you ready? We've got to go one hard, deep, huge, momentous, unimaginable step deeper. Because actually, in order to know that Mahsa Amini didn't die in vain, we have to go beyond the local experience of that particular tragic moment, and we need to place ourselves in the world context, and to understand that there are two tragic responses, **there are two ways to murder Eros.**

1. MURDERING EROS BY MEANS OF THE MORALITY POLICE

One way to murder Eros is through the morality police. When you murder Eros through the morality police, then you have those same police who rape women who are imprisoned, who rape young girls. Because they're split off from their own Eros, and they're shamed by their very existence; they experience themselves as being fundamentally bad. And once you experience yourself as fundamentally bad, there's no constraint; you've lost hope, you've lost a memory of your own future. And so paradoxically, and we've seen it in these protests, **the morality police become the rapists.** Wow! And so that's one tragic failure of Eros. And every breakdown of Eros brings a subsequent collapse of ethics. But that's not enough, friends.

2. MURDERING EROS BY MEANS OF THE SEX-NEUTRAL RESPONSE WHICH GENERATES THE PORNOGRAPHIC UNIVERSE

The second failure of Eros is the sex-neutral response that generates the pornographic universe. There's a second failure of Eros which brings its own collapse of ethics. **We're not complete, and we haven't honored She,**

unless we address that. And I want to say something here, and I want to go slow for a second. And it's deep and it's hard to say, but it needs to be said.

The secular liberal response, not the sex-negative response of fundamentalism, but the kind of bland sex-positive, or the sex-neutral response, that generates what I would call the pornographic universe, is equally—but in a completely different form—a murder of Eros.

This is not a moralistic position. And I want to understand this deeply. It's an understanding. It's not about "nakedness" in pornography, but about something much deeper.

The tragedy of the secular liberal order—when I say liberal, I don't mean liberal as opposed to conservative, I mean the secular postmodern Western liberal order that includes the preponderance of the mainstream, of the intellectual and media and social and entertainment establishments—**is a deconstruction of value.** And when we deconstruct value, we fail to realize the central value of Eros. Eros is no longer a value, because value doesn't exist, and we can't locate desire as a value.

Desire becomes "a random accident, engendered by random evolutionary survival," which is an embarrassment to our attempt to be a good citizen. This is why the liberal social order is producing a new puritanical culture that only understands violations of desire, that seeks to identify the great violators of desire—which is important.

We should identify, for example, sexual harassment, and have no tolerance for it, of course. We should identify the rape of men in prison and the rape of women all over the world, and have no tolerance for it, of course. We should step up and stand against any violation of Eros. **But the liberal**

social order has just stopped there. We've identified the violators of Eros, but we don't have a story of desire. We don't understand sex-erotic.

So therefore, we don't know how to return to Eros, because we don't understand that Eros is a value, and that we live in a CosmoErotic Universe. The sex-neutral narrative, the bland sex-positive narrative, or "sex is only sacred when we're procreating"—those become the narratives of the liberal social order.

But actually: **Desire is the currency of Life itself. Desire is Value.**

PORNOGRAPHY IS THE DECONTEXTUALIZATION OF RADICAL SEXING FROM RADICAL LIVING

What is pornography? Pornography is the decontextualization of radical sexing from radical living. We generate a pornographic universe, and **in this pornographic universe we decontextualize sex from story.** That's at the very core of a piece of writing we're doing to honor all the Mahsa Aminis in the world, called *The Phenomenology of Eros*. And in this *Phenomenology of Eros* that Dr. Kristina Kincaid and I are working on, we understand that pornography is not graphic sexual images.

If you look up pornography in the dictionary, you'll see "pornography is graphic sexual images." No.

Pornography is graphic sexual images that are isolated from the deep and gorgeous textured story of human desire.

And human desire means my whole life; my children, my values, my creativity, my ethos, my economics, my kindness, my Goodness, my Truth, my Beauty.

If you decontextualize sexual desire from the larger Field of Desire, if you take the graphic wonder of the sexual and you isolate it from the larger context of life, of a full life aflame with desire in every dimension of Reality—when you do that isolation, and you exile graphic sexuality from the larger story of a rich, textured, radically alive, dripping with desire, sacred autobiography in every dimension of life—*that's* pornography.

Pornography is the decontextualization of radical sexing from radical living. Wow, step one!

A PORNOGRAPHIC UNIVERSE VIOLATES THE GODDESS

And when we do that, we murder Eros. When we do that, we kill the Goddess. **When we generate a Reality in which ten-year-olds are plugged in to high-speed internet pornography**—before they even can understand the softness, the gentleness, the quivering tenderness, the fierceness, the goodness of Eros, as part of the larger life, the life of full desire in every dimension of life—**we violate the Goddess, we murder the Goddess, we murder Eros.**

But let's take it another step, and this other step is critical. And again, pornography is not graphic sexuality. **Pornography is addictive and destructive because it's isolated from the larger context of life.** Imagine you have a three-hour movie; a three-hour beautiful movie about depth and life and kindness and goodness and sensitivity and complexity and the agony and the ecstasy of a human life. And in that three-hour beautiful movie, you've got four minutes of radical sexing. Is that pornographic?

No, of course it's not, and it's also not addictive. Because it's sexing in the context of a life lived pulsing with desire, in which Eros and ethos are one. **It's only the decontextualization of those four minutes which exiles radical sexing from radical living.**

That's the pornographic, and that's the murder of Eros.

And let's go two more steps, and these two steps, I mean, they're so deep and they're so holy.

FUNDAMENTALIST TOTALITARIANISM AND PORNOGRAPHIC TOTALITARIANISM

There are two forms of totalitarianism in the world. I want to make a big and a huge leap here. There's a fundamentalist totalitarianism that seeks to eradicate all scripts of desire: all scripts of desire are eradicated, and Mahsa Amini is murdered because her hijab is tilted, and because the young men who murder her are shamed in the very depth and core of their being. That's one kind of totalitarianism.

There's a second kind of totalitarianism, which is a kind of pornographic totalitarianism. Now stay close.

> *In pornography, you don't access the depths of your own desire. Your desire is determined by commercial commodified scripts of desire that have been written for you.*

These are not your stories. This is not your imagination. This is not the sacred imagination of She living as Thee. This is not your unique depth of desire. This is not the unique texture of your configuration of intimacy and desire. None of this is you. **All of this is a violation of your Unique Self.**

You go to pornography, you watch one video, then the algorithmic structure of machine intelligence identifies your first kink. And then it sends you to a second one that looks like that, and to a third one, and then to a fourth one, and then to a fifth one. **And you get completely hijacked, you get completely drawn in**—out of yourself, out of your essential self, out of your inward space of desire—**into scripts of desire that have been written**

for you. Once the script of your desire is written for you, we're at the door of totalitarianism.

THE ONLY RESPONSE TO PORNOGRAPHIC TOTALITARIANISM IS YOUR OWN UNIQUE DESIRE

Freedom means you can trust yourself. Freedom means you can trust your body. Freedom means you can trust your desire. And the second that you can't trust your desire, and the second you can't trust your body, and the second you can't trust your Eros, then you have to give over authority of that Eros to someone else. That might be the morality police, or it might be a digital totalitarianism that imposes upon you, beyond the pale of awareness, the script of your desire that you naively claim as your own. But actually you've been through machine intelligence, defined by a set of statistical regularities of people watching the same kinds of porn, and **you keep receiving invitations to something which will take you deeper and deeper into that rabbit hole and farther and farther away from yourself.**

In other words, friends… **Both the morality police and the pornographic universe are rooted in the exile of desire, which is the exile of She, which is the exile of what the lineage calls the *Shekhinah*: the Goddess, Eros.**

When you exile She, when you exile desire, when you don't have access to your own desire which you can trust—to your own quality and configuration, to your own gorgeous queerness, to your own idiosyncratic story of desire—when you can't find that, but the script of your inner desire is written for you, we have already stepped into totalitarianism.

Let's go the last step friends, and it's so deep. It's so deep, and let's be in this together. **The only response to the pornographic universe**—whether it's the pornography of the morality police who are pornographic in their very being, or whether it's the pornography of a pornographic universe which is devoid of Eros—**is your own unique desire.**

The only thing more powerful than the impersonal pull of a depersonalized pornographic universe is the depth and intimacy of your own irreducibly unique story of desire. Your own story of desire.

THE NEW STORY OF VALUE: THE FULL POWER OF YOUR UNIQUE DESIRE

If you want to get the depth of this Reality construct, imagine if you can, for a second, this new Story of Value.

Imagine an electrical cord. At the end of the electrical cord is a plug. That plug is your unique Eros; that plug is your unique configuration of desire. That plug plugs into the Eros of Cosmos, the CosmoErotic Universe.

That's the actual scientific structure of Reality. Through your irreducible uniqueness, you plug into the socket, if you will, of Reality's electricity, Reality's electric Eros. And that electric Eros pours through your unique desire.

As long as you're what the MIT Media Lab calls *Homo imitans*, as long as you're imitating others—and for the MIT Media Lab, that's how you're supposed to be, and they're the people who are defining the internet today—**as long as you're imitating scripts of desire that have been provided for you**—that are in violation of your unique Eros, which is your Unique Self—**you have no energy; your energy is hijacked. You feel pallid and insipid; you feel empty, devastated, and depressed.**

The only antidote to the pornography of morality police and their murder of Eros, and to the pornographic universe which is split off from its own Eros, is the full power of your unique desire—which is your unique protest, which is your unique joy, which is your unique configuration of intimacy, which is your unique configuration of desire.

That's the new Story of Value. That's the new Story of Eros. That's the promise we make to Mahsa Amini: *you didn't die in vain.*

BARAYE: PROTESTING FOR THE SAKE OF THE ALL

Baraye: we live for the sake of it all.

Because we are omni-considerate for the sake of the whole. Because we are *Homo amor.* Because we're intimate with the whole. Because we're intimate with all of the future, and we're intimate with all of the present.

Mahsa Amini died with us and for us. And in Iran, they're protesting. And we're intimate with everything happening in Iran every single day. We're intimate with the tragedies of young men around the world who can't access their own powerful, erect expression of Eros.

To women who can't access the dignity of their own desire because they were trained in the murder of Eros—which is access to high-speed internet porn from the age of ten—and can't access the goodness and self-evident aliveness of being alive that the sexual gives us in her greatest and most wondrous expression.

So we're going to now protest one last time for the sake of the all, *Baraye.* And I invite everyone, as you read this, to pray. We're going to pray, and our prayer is *Baraye.* Here's our prayer. *Baraye,* means *for.*

What are we praying for?

For the sake of all the broken women, and for the sake of all the broken men. For the sake of my Uncle Henry who is having surgery. For the sake of health. For the sake of goodness.

Baraye, for the sake of it all.

41

CHAPTER THREE

FROM HOMO SAPIENS TO HOMO AMOR: RECLAIMING THE AUTHORSHIP AND AUTHORITY OVER OUR SCRIPTS OF DESIRE

Episode 319 — November 20, 2022

RECLAIMING THE SCRIPT OF MY UNIQUE DESIRE FROM TOTALITARIANISM

One of the things that I've talked about in the last twenty years, since writing a book called *Mystery of Love* in 2002, is being able to access the script of your own unique desire.

Fundamentalism on the one hand, and a broken liberal order on the other, seek to *rewrite* the script of desire. Fundamentalism *splits off* that script of desire, or even views that script of desire as being demonic—and not in a good way. But paradoxically, the pornographic universe *also* hijacks the scripts of desire. The pornographic universe is desire written *for* you — and not even by a group of vaudeville pornographers who wrote pornography in the 40s, and 50s, and 60s, and into the 70s.

Now scripts of desire are written by algorithmic machine intelligence, which decides which scripts receive the most hits, and what you watched, and how long your attention was in a particular moment of the pornographic universe, and then feeds you new invitations down that rabbit hole — which is not *your* desire.

The second I give up the writing of my own script of desire, and I allow somebody else to write the script of my desire, there is the beginning of totalitarianism. That's a big deal! When I allow others to write the script of my desire—others who seek commodification and short-term profit, who are misaligned with my own Unique Self, who don't recognize me, who organize algorithmic, machine-intelligence-driven reality to speak to the lowest common denominator of the human being, who upgrade algorithms in order to downgrade human beings, and who are living in a world of emergent upgraded algorithms and downgraded human beings that are unable to access unique desire—that's the beginning of totalitarianism. I have to access *my* unique desire.

Each one of us is an irreducibly unique expression of desire. And accessing unique desire is the antithesis of totalitarianism.

The second I allow someone else to write the script of my desire, that is the beginning of totalitarianism. Whether it's a regressive fundamentalism that's writing the script of my desire with the morality police *or* it's a broken liberal order that enacts a pornographic universe, both of them result in a degradation simply because it is *hijacking the script of my unique desire.*

What is my unique desire? My unique desire is my deepest heart's desire. Does that make sense? Can you *feel* it? When I say, *does that make sense,* I mean, *can you feel it in your body, your heart, and your mind? Can you feel it sensually?*

Sensemaking is sensual. When you know something is true, you know it because it's carnal knowledge, because you can feel it.

I can feel it in my body, in my heart, in my mind.

My heart's desire is the desire of my heart, my soul, my psyche, my body. I must write the great epic drama of my desire.

ALL DESIRE IS NON-LOCAL

My desire is *non-local* which means that my desire is *not just for me.* And it's also not just for me and my immediate family, no matter how beautiful they are, or how broken they are, or how much they exhaust me, or how much they take from me. Immediate family is important, and I have a great service there. Biology is not an accident. But actually, I can't serve my immediate family unless I'm serving the larger whole.

I need to know: Am I taking my seat at the table? Am I resting in my second innocence? Am I living the full joy of my being and becoming?

And from that place—when I am in my unique desire, in my deepest heart's desire, when I am giving my gift in my unique circle of intimacy and influence, when I am writing my unique letter in the cosmic scroll—I can be an incredible father, an incredible brother, an incredible son, an incredible sister, an incredible friend, and an incredible beloved, in all shapes, sizes, and forms of all kinds.

WE NEED TO RECOVER A MEMORY OF THE FUTURE

Imagine that you are Abraham, and you're hearing the call. And the call says *Lech-Lecha*: *go forth from the land, go forth from your father and mother's house.* Meaning, *leave the old traumas behind, leave the old story behind.*

We were all traumatized in different ways. As *Anna Karenina,* that great Russian novel, opens, *we all suffer uniquely, and we all suffer differently*—but we suffered trauma.

I've suffered enormous trauma in my life, unimaginable. And yet, I've got to *not* live in that, I've got to hold it, and do what I can to heal it and step into tomorrow. **But you can only recover from trauma when you stop living in the recursive loop of the *memory of yesterday* and allow yourself to be pulled by the strange attractor of the *memory of the future.***

Classical psychological work is important, but it obsesses over the past. It allows the psychological self to be hijacked by the past. *When I am hijacked by the past, when I view my work of recovery as recovering the memories of the past, then I can never live in the present or access the future.*

To *recover* is to recover a memory of the future. And the memory of the future is recovered by one organ of the human body: the heart/soul, *which is the organ of desire.*

DESIRE REACHES FOR THE FUTURE

Desire, by its very nature, reaches for the future. We are *Homo desirous*— we are human beings who desire. We are *Homo prospectus*—we are prospecting, for the gold, for the vision, for the shimmering invitation of a new future.

My teacher, Nachman of Breslov, was one of the great inspirations for Franz Kafka. He said three words in Aramaic, that when you get up in the morning, the very first act you do as *Homo amor*, he called it *Zichron Alma De'Atid*: you remember the future.

We become intimate not *just* with the past, not *just* with the split-off parts of ourselves. We do need to become intimate with the split-off parts of ourselves and that's what a Unique Self encounter is: when you have lost a part of yourself and I am holding it and I return it to you. We are not *just* intimate with our split-off parts, but even more than that, we are intimate with the future.

We hear the call of the future. Who do we need to be in five years from now? In the fashion of *Groundhog Day,* are we going to keep repeating the same day again and again? This is what most of us do most of the time. Most people over most of the world, most of the time, keep living the same day again and again.

In the words of Macbeth, *because tomorrow, and tomorrow, and tomorrow creeps in this petty pace from day to day to the last syllable of recorded time…*

we fall into extinction and dystopia. Will it be *tomorrow, and tomorrow, and tomorrow...* that bursts the memory of my personal future? Or will we break through to tomorrow?

WHAT IS YOUR DEEPEST HEART'S DESIRE?

So, I want to—with permission, friends, tenderly, vividly, audaciously, humbly—I want to ask you a question, the most personal question in the world. The most personal question in the world is not about your money or your sex. The most personal question in the world is:

What is your deepest heart's desire that you know is omni-considerate for the sake of the whole?

Not your deepest heart's desire as a separate self, but your deepest heart's desire as Evolutionary Unique Self, playing your instrument in the Unique Self Symphony as *Homo sapiens* who has become *Homo amor*. Find your desire from that place and *know that your unique desire is the desire of Cosmos, discreetly expressed in you.*

Friends, we live in a pornographic universe. The pornographic universe isn't just about Pornhub, or pornographic channels. The whole thing is a pornographic universe. The way the news is run is a pornographic universe. The way CNN is run and the way Fox News is run are different versions of the pornographic universe.

Everything is driven by a commodified profit to arrest your attention for a short amount of time, to emerge your surface pathos, to then give you a feeling of surface catharsis, and then you go on with business as usual, *reliving the same day again and again.*

No! We've got to move from the pornographic universe to the CosmoErotic Universe, to a CosmoErotic Humanism. And *humanism* means your *unique humanity*, which is your *unique desire*.

Because who are we? We are unique incarnations of intimacy and desire. And as we become *Homo amor*, we can actually begin a great wave. That wave is going to start with a trickle, it's going to start with a rivulet, it's going to start with a few drops. They are going to gather force, and they are going to come together, and we are going to find each other. *My arousal, and my water, and my rivulet, and my trickle are going to find your trickle.* And soon we are going to come together as a mighty river, and flood the world with the waters of creativity, of caring, of kindness, the waters of Goodness, of Truth, and of Beauty.

RECLAIMING THE DIGNITY OF NEED

We are afraid to talk about need. We are afraid that if we need each other, we're codependent. Or if we need each other, we don't really love each other because we need something from each other.

We *all* need each other. To say *I love you*, that's to say *I need you*. If I am willing to let you love me, I need to know that you need me. We need each other. We need each other as Unique Self Symphony. We need each other in our dyads and in our triads. We need to become a band of Outrageous Lovers.

On the inside of the inside, who are we? We are a band of Outrageous Lovers. We are *Homo sapiens*, madly committed to each other and to becoming *Homo amor*, to evoke this moment in human history. We are *Homo sapiens* becoming *Homo amor*: a Planetary Awakening in Love through Unique Self Symphonies.

CHAPTER FOUR

THE RESPONSE TO EXISTENTIAL AND CATASTROPHIC RISK IS THE DAWN OF DESIRE

Episode 362 — September 17, 2023

EVOLUTIONARY LOVE CODE: THE DAWN OF DESIRE

There are three classical responses to the meta-crisis:

1. The Doomer Response
2. The Denial Response
3. The Domination Response

None of these three can avert the meta-crisis. Each of them deepens what is sure to be its devastating impact, its devastating suffering.

There is however a fourth response: the Dawn of Desire or, said slightly differently, the Dawn of Desire and its Dignities, or the Dawn of Desire and its Divinities—living uniquely in us, as us, and through us, both personally and in our newly emergent Unique Self Symphonies.

This is the new grammar of value, the core First Principles and First Values embedded in a Story of Value—a story of desire which is the great new story, the new cultural movement of CosmoErotic Humanism. It is only such a new Story of Value, such an emergent CosmoErotic Humanism, that can generate the evolutionary intimacy, the new order of intimacy,

that responds to the global intimacy disorder that itself is the root cause of the meta-crisis.

CosmoErotic Humanism tells the story of ErosValue. CosmoErotic Humanism tells the story of DesireValue. CosmoErotic Humanism is the dawn of new possibility—the possibility of desire.

FOUR RESPONSES TO EXISTENTIAL AND CATASTROPHIC RISK

Existential risk takes two forms. One is an actual extinction: *the death of humanity as we know it.* There are about twelve vectors at play quite seriously today that could bring us there, if there is no deep intervention.

The second kind of existential risk is the death of *our* humanity. By the death of our humanity we mean a creeping, benign totalitarianism—what we refer to as TechnoFeudalism—in which the world becomes encased in a kind of Skinner box, where free will, personhood, and human dignity are undermined without our even being *aware* that that's happening. Catastrophic risk is not the death of humanity or the death of our humanity, but it involves large-scale unimaginable suffering to large swaths of humanity and to the animal world.

There are three classical responses to existential and catastrophic risk.

1. THE DOOMER RESPONSE

The doomer response means, in a word, *it's over.* The doomer community includes people like Joanna Macy, or my old colleague Michael Dowd, who wrote a book called *Thank God for Evolution*, but has since become a doomer. The doomer community is one of the most intelligent, well-read communities in the world, and they have come to the conclusion—based on books like *Overshoot*, which is one of their classical texts—that *it's too late. We have breached too many planetary boundaries;, there is nothing more that can be done.* The doomer move says, *you've got to just grieve the end.* Again, these are not superficial readers. These are people who have read a lot, who have come to a conclusion that there is actually no hope.

The doomer community is rooted in subtle reductive materialism. For example, my friend Michael Dowd's book, *Thank God for Evolution* is suffused with subtle reductive materialism dressed up as Spirit. I was worried about the book then, that it wouldn't *hold* in the face of massive crisis.

There is this subtle reductive materialism—*possibility is over*—that lines the doomer community. While I appreciate and can feel the impulse, it's ultimately wrong, because it doesn't understand a critical point. The same possibility that moved Reality in the first nanoseconds of the Big Bang, and moved us from matter to life to mind, that *same* evolutionary impulse— which is the inherent *telos* of Reality, the directionality of Reality—is alive *today.* Evolution itself is the Possibility of Possibility. That's lost on the doomer community.

2. THE DENIAL RESPONSE

The second position, which I would say is the most rampant position, is denial. The denial position has two forms: what I would call *conscious* denial, and more the sloppy or *unconscious* denial.

Conscious denial is: you are familiar with some of the facts, but you just turn away. You're not willing—to borrow Robert J. Lifton's phrase—*to face apocalypse* or to face the possibility of existential risk, so you turn away. It's a turning away. It's a turning away of the face. It's a deliberate turning away, burying the face in the sand.

I remember when my dear friend Sean Raymer—whom I met when I was giving about a decade of wisdom schools at a retreat center in New York— said to me: *Why are we talking about this? It's hopeless, what can we do about it?* His impulse was, *let's just turn away from this.*

Marc, teach us about Unique Self, teach us about your new visions of enlightenment—why are you talking about the meta-crisis? I started talking about the meta-crisis intensely in 2010 and 2011. That's when existential risk became more real than real to me, and I called it then *the second shock of existence*, the shock of the potential death of humanity.

Sean was basically saying, *there is just no point.* Sean wasn't, of course, advocating denial. It wasn't a *negative* denial: he was just saying that *there is no point in engaging this, there is nothing to say.* That's pretty much what all intelligent people said to me as I started talking about this: *What are you talking about? First off, you are probably wrong, and even if you're right, what's there to do about it?*

There are many shades of denial. There is a conscious denial: you know the facts, you deny them, because you don't know what to do about it. And then there's a second, more sloppy, unconscious denial, where you get a whiff of it, you can taste it, you feel a fragrance of it in the air—and you turn away. That's where most of the world is.

Take, for example, artificial intelligence. You read something in a passing headline about artificial intelligence being an existential risk. I talked about this five or six years ago, at a bunch of talks in Belgium. Everyone laughed. All of a sudden, in the last four months [October 2023], you read in mainstream newspapers that artificial intelligence is an existential risk.

But people turn away, because *how can you talk about that?* People read the newspaper, and they say: *Oh my God, artificial intelligence could be an existential risk,* and then they go on with their lives, because they don't know how to hold it. It's a *casual* denial. That's the second approach.

3. THE DOMINATION RESPONSE

The third approach to the meta-crisis is domination. I would call that the approach of Elon Musk. Elon has looked at a lot of the data that I've looked at. There are, in our world, some overlapping people. We've looked at a lot of the same data, and Elon has absolutely come to the same conclusion about the reality of the meta-crisis and existential risk. But Elon's response is domination. (And I don't think it's a malevolent response.) Elon's response is something like: *There are no adults in the room. Governments are all short-termers. No one's looking at the big picture. I've got to take responsibility and be an adult in the room.*

Now, Elon is—as Walter Isaacson pointed out in his biography—both an adult and a child, and a complex figure. This is not a discussion on Elon. Blessings to Elon. Elon is trying to be an adult in the room, and he's saying, *Domination; I'm going to run the show.*

If you want to know why Musk bought Twitter, it was part of an overarching play that's connected to Tesla, and that's connected to his satellites that encircle the globe, and to an entire neural link system, which is related to what I would call the death of *our* humanity, where an invisible group of controllers dominate and control the systems that are trans-governmental. Elon represents a certain version of a domination move, which from his perspective is benign. But of course, **all domination moves begin as benign.**

Those are the three basic moves: The first is the denial move, the second is the doomer move, and the third is the domination move. None of those moves will work. All three of those moves not only will not solve the meta-crisis. Rather, they will deepen the unimaginable suffering of the meta-crisis, and will eventually lead either to the death of humanity or to the death of *our* humanity—one of those two forms—or to unimaginable forms of catastrophic risk.

4. THE DESIRE RESPONSE

There has to be a fourth way, and that fourth way is not denial, it's not doomer, it's not domination. It is what we might call the ***Dawn of Desire***— And yes, it had to be a D, double D, because D's are always new beginnings: decisive, directional—that's D's at their best; D's at their best begin new things. There's this new, decisive direction, which we're going to call the *Dawn of Desire*, or the Dawn of Desire and Her Dignities, and the Dawn of Desire and Her Divinities. I want to talk about this Dawn of Desire because this is the fourth way. And this Dawn of Desire is the new story of CosmoErotic Humanism.

THE FOURTH RESPONSE TO THE META-CRISIS: THE DAWN OF DESIRE

This new code, this code of Cosmos, is a new formulation of the new Story of Value, which is CosmoErotic Humanism. This is the fourth response to the meta-crisis: the Dawn of Desire.

You cannot respond to the meta-crisis only by changing the infrastructure, for example, by changing how we detect bioweapons in the wastewater (although we need to do that, absolutely). You cannot respond to the meta-crisis only by changing the social structure, enacting new laws.

We do *also* need new laws and new ways of engaging, for example, technology. Laws are based on precedent, while technology is ever-new and emergent, and precedent law can't actually engage the new and the emergent. This is one of many reasons that law has been unable to bind technology.

But social structure is insufficient. We need a new superstructure. A new *superstructure* is a new grammar of value: inherent First Principles and First Values of Cosmos embedded in a Story of Value. Let's break that down.

SEEING THE STORYLINE: FROM UNCONSCIOUS TO CONSCIOUS EVOLUTION

Reality is a story. Story is not a human contrivance. It's not a made-up idea. There is an *ontology* to story. Yes, human beings are storytelling animals, but not because that's some random social expression. Human beings are storytelling animals because human beings are the human expression of a Cosmos that *is* story.

Reality is always story, and the movement from unconscious to conscious evolution is when we become conscious of the story: conscious of the fact that we incarnate the story, conscious of the fact that the story is an unfinished story, conscious of the fact that we become storytellers of the new story. That's the move from unconscious to conscious evolution.

UNCONSCIOUS EVOLUTION

Unconscious evolution is an unconscious story. You can identify the storyline only from the later perspective of conscious evolution. An atom is living in a particular story, and that story is a Story of Value.

There is a set of values that govern the atomic, subatomic, molecular, and macro-molecular worlds. The reason atoms come together to form a molecule is because they have a shared Field of Value. That's the language of Cosmos.

Cosmos is multiple forms of language. Language is embedded in Cosmos, even as we are embedded in language. One of the core structures of the interior sciences—which we have developed in CosmoErotic Humanism— is the language of value, which is the structure of Cosmos. That language of value goes all the way down the evolutionary chain. It drives evolution. It's innate, inherent, and it evolves.

CONSCIOUS EVOLUTION

The cosmological story comes alive when we become *aware* of the story, when we can actually *see* the story. We can see: *Oh my God, Oh my Goddess, there is a narrative arc to Cosmos, there is a storyline.*

Being able to see the storyline, to detect the storyline, is itself the movement from unconscious to conscious evolution.

The story becomes conscious:

- It becomes conscious in me; I realize: *I am the story.*
- I realize the story is unfinished: *I've got to write the next chapter of the story.*
- I write the next chapter of the story by *being* the next chapter of the story.
- Finally, I *become* the storyteller. Wow!

NEED AND DESIRE ARE ISOMORPHIC AT FUNDAMENTAL AND ASPIRATIONAL LEVELS OF EVOLUTION

What is the new story about? It's a story of desire. And what is desire? Desire is the erotic motive of Cosmos. Cosmos *is* Desire. Desire *is* the nature of Reality. That's what evolution is: Evolution is desire. Now, desire desires value. Value is clarified desire. Clarified desire desires to express itself as *value.*

At the fundamental levels of evolution, value is innate. When atoms are in a shared Field of Value, there is an impulse within atoms to become a molecule. In the same way, let's go back a little bit farther, closer to the Big Bang, about 380,000 years after the Big Bang, there is an inherent desire in subatomic particles to create larger wholes. They share this inherent desire for this larger value, and that value is called an atom. The desire of subatomic particles to become an atom is their core need, because at that level, **at that fundamental level of Cosmos, there is no split between *need* and *desire*.** Need and desire are the same.

Need and desire remain virtually isomorphic—virtually identical—through virtually every level of the world of matter, the *physiosphere.* And then the world of matter triumphs in the Second Big Bang, which is the *biosphere.* In the biosphere, again, there is this desire for more value.

- More value means more *life.*

- More value means more *uniqueness*.
- More value means more *Eros*.
- More value means more *creativity*.
- More value means more *intimacy*.

Each one of those is a precise word that we've articulated in CosmoErotic Humanism, and formulated an interior science equation to talk about them.

Again, need and desire are exactly the same at these levels of evolution. Now, at some point, we go through all the levels of the biosphere, and we get to the savanna and the human being, *Homo erectus*, gradually emerges. We are standing up straight. And at some point—it's debatable when, and there is an argument between historians—but at some point around 75,000–400,000 years ago, two new dimensions emerge at virtually the same time: one is language, and the other is art, aesthetics. From those comes trade, and there's this new Third Big Bang, life triumphs in the depths of the self-reflective human, in—to borrow a word from Vladimir Vernadsky, the Russian cosmist, *the noosphere*—the world of culture, ideas, transmittable ideas. The next step emerges, which is allowed for through language and through art and through trade, but language is the core.

As the human emerges, there is an apparent split between need and desire. *My needs are what I really need, and desire is what I just desire.* **That's only an apparent split. It disappears when I go deeper inside and clarify what I *truly* need and what I *truly* desire.**

Not *what are my surface desires*, *my pseudo-desires*, or—using the language of CosmoErotic Humanism—not *what's the pseudo-eros* that covers over the emptiness. But rather the question is: **what's the core Eros, which is my core need and core desire?** Eros means desire. Eros is what Alfred North Whitehead, who wrote *Principia Mathematica* with George Bertrand Russell, called the *appetition* of Cosmos. Cosmos has *appetite*, Cosmos has desire.

> *The desire of Cosmos, at the level of the self-reflective human, is able to enact a new possibility, which is a higher level, a deeper level of choice.*

I begin to choose, and I begin to be able to discern between my *pseudo-desire* and my *true* desire—what I called, together with my beloved evolutionary whole mate, Barbara Marx Hubbard—your *deepest heart's desire.*

Your deepest heart's desire is actually your *clarified* desire. It's the Dawn of Desire. **Your clarified desire is the realization that the evolutionary impulse, which is evolutionary desire, lives uniquely *in you, as you, and through you.*** You are, I am, we are clarified desire. I am no longer merely *Homo sapiens,* who is told by the religions:

> *Conquer your desire because we don't trust you to get your true desire.*
> *We are afraid of your pseudo-desires.*
> *We are going to tell you what you desire.*
> *You can't trust your body—we will tell you what your body can do.*
> *We will tell you what you're allowed to desire, and you are allowed to desire what we tell you is desirable.*

That's the beginning of oppression. It was perhaps, in part, a necessary stage in culture, but we now need to transcend that. We need to be at the dawn of a new age of desire, a new possibility of desire, in which the human being begins once again to realize:

Who am I?

1. I am the CosmoErotic Universe in person.
2. I am evolutionary desire in person.
3. Evolution *is* desire.
4. Evolution lives uniquely in me, as me, and through me.
5. I am a unique incarnation of evolutionary desire.

I AM A UNIQUE FEATURE OF THE FIELD OF DESIRE

My desire is the desire of *She*. It is the desire of Cosmos. It is Goddess's desire. It's God's desire. It's Reality's desire. It is the telos of Reality itself, living both in me personally and in us collectively—in me as an irreducible Unique Self, and in us as Unique Selves coming together in Unique Self Symphony.

Unique Self is not merely the separate self who is a skin-encapsulated ego, who we can't rely on to trust their desire, because the skin-encapsulated ego, the separate self, was lost in the optical delusion of separateness where *I see everything as rivalrous conflict governed by win/lose metrics, and my desire seems to be always at the expense of your desire, and I've got to be in competition with you because I'm trying to survive. And it's me against you, in a zero-sum competition.*

I've got to *trance-end* that—to *end* that *trance*, to realize I am True Self, I am *one* with the Field of Desire—and then **I've got to realize that Field of Desire is *seamless* but not *featureless*, so that I am Unique Self: I am that Field of Desire's unique feature.** Who am I?

I am a unique configuration of desire. That's who I am.

> *I am a unique configuration of desire, and my unique desire is needed by Cosmos.*

At this level, need and desire come back together. **Just like for subatomic particles, need and desire are isomorphic, for the new human and new humanity**—the fulfillment of *Homo sapiens* as *Homo amor*, who understands him/herself as being Unique Self, a unique discretion of True Self, a unique discretion of the Field of Desire, a unique configuration of desire, needed by All-That-Is—**the clarified desire and the clarified need are precisely the same.**

CLARIFIED DESIRE EQUALS VALUE, AND MY CLARIFIED DESIRE IS UNIQUE

I've got to begin to trust my desire, to trust my body. I've got to clarify my desire.

Clarified desire equals value. That's what value is. Desire is a desire for a new value, for a future that's not yet here. Can you feel that? That's what desire is. Do you get how gorgeous that is?

Clarified desire equals value, and my clarified desire is unique, and so I have a unique contribution to make to the shared Field of Value.

THE DIGNITY OF DESIRE

We talked about Mahsa Amini who was brutally killed in Iran. We played a song: "Baraye," "For The Sake Of." Mahsa Amini was an expression of *She*, of the Field of Desire, of the feminine. The feminine wants to take its scarf off. She wants to not just be seen through the scarf's slit.

The West is often the opposite, where there is a *degradation* of dress, without tastefulness, without holding the beauty and the subtlety of dress. That's a Western degradation, one of the shadows of Western freedom. But the other degradation of the world is the *covering up* of desire, and the degradation of *She*, the degradation of the divinity and dignity of desire. That's what Mahsa Amini stood for. She stood for the dignity of desire.

There is a song that's going around in Iran today, a year after Mahsa Amini passed. This is a song about the dignity of desire:

> *Take off your scarf, the sun is sinking!*
> *Take off your scarf, your pleasant perfume fills the air.*

Take off your scarf, let your hair flow!
Don't be afraid, my love! Laugh, protest against tears!
Take off your scarf, let your hair flow!
Don't be afraid, my love! Laugh, protest against tears!
The dance of red tresses, the lump in my throat, all your hair.
My face gets wet, I get your wish.
Take off your scarf, make the air bright and fresh!
My love, don't be afraid, dance, boldly bend to kiss!
Take off your scarf, make the air bright and fresh!
My love, don't be afraid, dance, boldly bend to kiss!
Take off your scarf, the sun is sinking.
Woman, Life, Freedom
Woman, Life, Freedom

CLARIFYING OUR DESIRE IN RESPONSE TO THE META-CRISIS

The fourth response to the meta-crisis is to clarify our desire.

- Is it our clarified desire that we live lives filled with dread and emptiness?
- Is it our clarified desire that we cannot access our deepest heart's desire?
- Is it our clarified desire that we are alienated from our desire for community and communion?
- Is it our clarified desire that we cannot access our desire to be omni-responsible for the whole, to feel and care for past, present, and future, to love the unborn future generations?
- Is it our clarified desire that we cannot access our sacred will to create a world in which there's not two billion vulnerable people who are split off from basic human dignity and human rights?
- Is our desire reducible to the lowest common denominator?

In order to feed that lowest-common-denominator frenzy of the hungry ghost—which needs to consume and consume and consume—**we develop an extraction model which extracts from planet Earth the resources that took billions of years to create.**

This is an indication of a frenzy of pseudo-desire—driving exponential growth curves that ultimately are guaranteed to fall off—that's lowest common denominator, *un-clarified* desire.

The response to the meta-crisis is to generate a new Story of Value in which we live. And a new Story of Value comes from only one place: clarified desire.

It's not denial. It's not doom. It's not domination. It's the dawn of desire.

What's the Dawn of Desire?

- It's the dawn of the *dignity* of desire.
- It's the dawn of *clarified* desire.
- It's the realization of the *divinity* of desire.
- It's our capacity to access our *deepest heart's desire.*
- It's the new story of CosmoErotic Humanism.

The new story of CosmoErotic Humanism is "*I become desire in person.*" *Homo amor* is the CosmoErotic Universe in person; *Homo amor* is Evolutionary Desire in person.

And I've got to be able to *trust* my desire:

I trust my clarified desire.
I trust my deepest heart's desire.
I trust the deepest dignity of my desire, rooted as it is in the ultimate divinity of desire.

The fourth response to the meta-crisis is the recognition of our desire—clarified desire, our deepest heart's desire—as disclosing the true nature of value in Cosmos. **The fourth response to the meta-crisis is to reclaim the dignity of desire in every unique human being.** And from that shared Field of Desire, to create new intimate communions and new Unique Self Symphonies; to create, to generate the new world for the new human and new humanity, *Homo sapiens* fulfilled as *Homo amor*:

- Trusting, clarifying our deepest heart's desire, being willing to go deep into our bodies, deep into our traumas, deep into our brokenness, and know that we can trace it back to its root—and find our goodness, and find our truth, and find our beauty.

- Knowing that the only recourse is not to *control* a human being because we falsely believe that they're empty of the Field of Desire and its dignities and its divinities—which is the doomer response, which is the domination response, and it's also part of the denial response. The denial response says, *I'm going to deny because there's nothing to do.* Yes, of course there's something to do. *Of course* there is something to do. What's there to do? Tell and *be* the new Story of Value. Move from unconscious to conscious evolution.

I am done being just *Homo sapiens.*

I am done being just a *separate self.*

I am done with the *degradation* of my desires.

I am going to begin to *trust* my somatic intelligence, to trust my deepest embodiment, my deepest ensoulment. I can trust that.

I can trust the personal myth that has awakened alive in me. That personal myth that is me is not a myth in the small sense. It is my deepest heart's desire. It is a personal story of desire, because my story is a story of desire.

That's what the new story is. It is the story of the *desire that we trust*, and of our *collective desires that we trust*, which are not the short-term desires of the political structures and the economic structures that are built in rivalrous conflict, governed by win/lose metrics, that produce a world of brokenness.

DESIRE IS PRAYER, PRAYER IS DESIRE

Prayer is to turn into the Field of Desire, to the Personhood and the Infinity of Desire—to the Infinity of Intimacy, which is the Field of Desire—and say:

Oh my God, help me, hold me.

I hold You, and I help You.

We are partners with the infinite Field of Desire. We are partners with the Goddess. We are partners with *She*. I want to invite everyone to the Field of Desire, and to pray by expressing your deepest heart's desire—for yourself, for your life, for your own humanity, for other people whose desires need fulfillment, for the desire of humanity. I want to offer you a new way to pray, with your permission, so tenderly.

To say I desire is to say I pray.
To say I pray is to say I desire.

Do you see how that changes what we think about prayer and how we feel prayer? Prayer has become this outmoded structure to a homophobic, anti-body, ethnocentric God that is somehow alienated from Cosmos. No!

The Field of *She* holds Cosmos and holds me.

Every place I fall, I fall into *Her* arms. *She* knows my name.

She lives in me, as me, and through me, and I *participate* in *She* at the same time.

To pray means one thing: Prayer is *pallal*. *Pallal* means "to consider the nature of Reality." And how do we consider the nature of Reality? I find my deepest heart's desire.

REALITY IS THE DESIRE FOR EVER MORE EROSVALUE

My deepest heart's desire always is value.

Reality is the desire for ever more value. Evolution is the evolution of desire, which is the evolution of intimacy, which is the evolution of value.

It is not that Eros *is* a value. It's *ErosValue*. Just like there is *LoveIntelligence*, and *LoveBeauty*, and *LoveDesire* (these are signatures of CosmoErotic Humanism), so there is *ErosValue*, there is *DesireValue*. It's one word.

Trust your deepest heart's desire. Find your deepest heart's desire. I find my deepest heart's desire. We collectively find our deepest heart's desire.

What's our deepest heart's desire? **We take the baton of the past, and we stand with every human being and with all of life in the present, and we hear the call of the unborn of the future.** We are in revolution and we are in *evolution*. We are evolution in person.

Desire rages in us—clarified desire. That's who we are. We are clarified desire. We are the dawn of the new desire.

We are at a moment of meta-crisis. The doomer response will destroy us. The denial response will destroy us. The domination response will destroy us. We have to choose a fourth response, which is a new decision we have to take. It's a decision about the Dignity and Divinity of Desire. The Dawn of Desire: as you, as me, as She, as we.

CHAPTER FIVE

THE DEGRADATION OF DESIRE— DISCERNING THE ISRAEL AND HAMAS CONFLICT: EVOLVING THE BATTLE OF GOOD & EVIL TO A HIGHER LEVEL OF CONSCIOUSNESS

Episode 365 — October 8, 2023

Editor's note: This episode was broadcast immediately after the events of October 7, 2023 and prior to the entry of the Israel Defense Forces to Gaza several weeks later.

Israel has always gone to supreme efforts to avoid innocent casualties, in line with the Israel Defense Forces' code of ethical standards which holds itself to more stringent ethical standards than any other army in the world. In spite of this, Hamas' total disregard for the wellbeing of the Gazan people and their cynical use of the Gazan people as political pawns has tragically caused untold and unnecessary heartbreak, suffering, and death on both sides, including much tragic unavoidable collateral damage to innocent Gazan civilians, which of course we feel intimately, decry, and mourn.

HOW DO YOU BEGIN A CONVERSATION?

This is a difficult day, and it's hard to know how to begin. I want to try and find our way here, and understand where we are—not by giving a political analysis of the day: the tragedy, the horror that's unfolding in

Israel (although we will talk about that). There is no political analysis that is separate from—that is in any way *distinguishable* from—the deeper conversation that we've been having here.

I was up all night, I didn't sleep. My son Yair has been here with me. Yair is an incredibly beautiful young man. The qualities that are so missing in much of the sophisticated cultural conversation, he incarnates all of them in spades. He is sincere in this incredible way. He experiences—and he has an incarnation of—devotion. He is filled with integrity. He's kind. He's generous. He has a heart that overflows. He has been a commander of commandos in different positions in the Israeli army. He is now in his early 30s, which in the Israeli army is ancient.

To get a sense of what's going on: he was called back to his unit, to his boys, and at about 3am, I walked him to a car service that we ordered to pick him up here in the Northeast Kingdom of Vermont, to take him to Burlington to get an 11 o'clock flight to Israel, in order to join the fighting.

Back in 2008, my other son Eytan was visiting me in Salt Lake City. Myself, Eytan, Diane Hamilton, and Michael Zimmerman, we spent a beautiful Sabbath talking in the depth of the snow of Utah. I was so thrilled to have Eytan with me. It was at a heartbreaking moment in my life.

And then, an earlier Gaza conflict broke out. Eytan left after being with me for thirty-six hours. Again, I walked him to a car, to a cab, and he flew back to Israel. He went directly into battle. He was also a commander of commandos. He went directly into battle, a house-to-house battle in Gaza in which many Israeli soldiers were killed because the Israeli army has followed a code of ethics in a situation which is beyond impossible.

I've researched this my entire life, and I've never seen any army come close to this code of ethics. They give full warning in every possible way, to clear civilians out of the way of operations, which are designed to stop what is pure terrorism. It's not anything other than that, and that needs to be understood, and I'm going to explain what that means. Eytan has described to me what happens when you go into a house, and you try and clear people out: you walk into the house and you'll have a baby put in front of you. The soldier steps back because the soldier is trained in ethics and doesn't want to hurt a baby. And in that stepping back, the soldier is often killed.

Eytan left my house and went into Gaza. He never talks about it, but in those two weeks, he was essentially on the ground, heavily armed, trying to navigate a deep existential threat to Israel's existence.

I read this morning the Charter of Hamas. Everyone should take a look at it, you can find it online. Hamas is aligned with Iran—Iran that's been involved in the last year in the slaughter of its own women teenagers, for daring to assert their autonomy as women, as human beings. We've talked about what's happened in the last year in Iran.

Iran, representing the most brutal repression of the feminine, of Eros, of goodness, truth, and beauty, is actually responsible for the activities of Hezbollah in the North border of Israel, for all of the terrorist cells on the West Bank of Israel, for the terrorist cells in Lod and Ramallah in central Israel (which is a tiny country), and for an extensive Hamas terror organization in Gaza.

Hamas' commitment is to have no negotiated settlement, no peace, no sharing of land, no shared story of value, no possibility of coexistence. Just read the charter of Hamas. The charter is clear that only the annihilation of Israel and only the restoration of the entire region as an Islamic state, only their triumph—based on the most fundamentally human-violating principles of the most repressive and ugly versions of medieval Islam—will satisfy the Prophet.

A little shocking! It's like, wow! How do you even begin a conversation?

EROS AND ETHICS ARE THE SAME THING

The first thing that we have to say is: my son was in Gaza for two weeks, and he wrote then that he didn't expect to leave Gaza alive. He hasn't talked about it since.

He left Gaza alive after two weeks, he was shocked. When he left Gaza and returned to the marketplace in Jerusalem, he was shocked that the ordinary world still existed. And then a couple of days later—just the explosive nature of the entire situation and almost the inability to hold it in the body—he was in a car accident, and wound up in Tel Hashomer hospital, and I got a call saying that he would never walk again. Eytan is fierce like his brother Yair, and is filled with goodness, and integrity, and generosity, and fight—deep, deep fight and a deep commitment. Eytan not only decided he was going to walk again, but multiple operations later, he has run ten marathons around the world competitively, and opened an educational institution in Israel, which trains people in good thinking and good moral thinking and philosophy through running, through training and running. So yay, Eytan!

That was the last time I walked my son in 2008 to a battle, and now we just walked Yair—I just want to share the context with you—Yair got on a plane at about 6:30, connecting to Israel. Mad blessings to Yair, and mad blessings to every single person in Israel; every single man, woman, and child.

I want to try and talk about this in a way that actually *begins* to do sensemaking. Because you cannot talk about this without all of the larger issues that we've been discussing.

The situation in Israel, it's so unbearably painful, just like the situation in Ukraine is so unbearably painful, and we have to *not* look away. **We need to look towards Israel, and we need to look towards the very fabric of the social, existential, spiritual fabric of Reality, and understand what is actually happening here.**

IN THE FIELD OF EROSVALUE

First, we cannot talk about this without establishing a Field of Value in which value is *real* and there is a *shared ground* of value, a shared grammar of value, and that there is some sense in which value is not just made-up.

It's not just a political creation, it's not just a social construction. **We *align* with value; *value lives in us.***

We have to listen deeply and clarify our interior to listen to the voice of value, to which we have direct access, and we can trust our direct access to that value that lives inside. That value lives inside every human being, and we can listen to that voice of value and trust it, and trust it as it moves in us—as the mysteries live within us. We cannot talk about this without that possibility, without that shared ground of value in which we participate, which lives in us, as us, and through us.

It is value which both evolves through us and at the same time, we bow before it. We bow before value. We bow before the mystery. We encounter the mystery, and the mystery incarnates as value, as goodness, as truth, as beauty, as the field of ethos and Eros, which is one.

Eros is the experience of radical aliveness, seeking, desiring deeper contact and greater wholeness, and that means that Eros and ethics are the same thing. Ethics is the experience of radical aliveness seeking, desiring ever deeper contact and ever greater wholeness. That's what ethos is. There is no split between Eros and ethics.

We are committed to creating, generating, fostering, supporting a Field of Eros and ethos that supports all of life. That is the ground for any conversation. Without that ground, we can't have a conversation.

EVERY RELIGION MUST EVOLVE

There are better and worse expressions of Eros and ethos. There is no moral equivalence. You can't just erase any notion of distinction. You have to be willing to do the deep work of collecting truth. Yes, there are multiple perspectives when people have an argument, but not infinite perspectives. You have to actually collect information—facts. It's got to be about the facts. Facts means there is something that's real, there is something that's empirical, that's checkable.

When you are on the playground, and the bully punches you, and you punch back, there is a distinction between the punching back and the original punch. They are not the same. How things come about when someone comes into your house to rape your daughter, and you defend your daughter, and you kill them because that was the only way to save your daughter—that's not murder, that's something else. That is killing in defense of the Field of Value.

I had a conversation with the Dalai Lama when I was in Dharamsala. We talked about this notion of utter moral equivalence and how devastating it is. There must be no moral equivalences.

There is a gentleman who writes in the United States, whom I have not tracked closely. His name is Sam Harris. I've listened to five or six of his presentations, and I take issue with some core assumptions that he makes that I think are flawed. But on one issue, I think he's done a brilliant job—and this is actually where I encountered his work, maybe a decade ago—where he did the completely audacious thing of challenging Islam, and challenging this notion of moral equivalence in which you weren't allowed to critique the way Islam was expressing itself in the world. He was right.

The fact is—and this is a tragic fact but a true fact—every religion has its text that it should be embarrassed by. **Every religion has a shadow.** That's absolutely true. And every religion needs to evolve in accordance with its own values, in order to align with the broader Field of Value.

What do I mean by that? For example, in the Torah, which is the sacred text of Judaism, there is a set of texts that talk about the injunction to kill everyone when the Israelites conquer ancient Canaan. That's tragic, and that was the nature of the ancient world. A few hundred years later, about 2,500 years ago, the readers of that text said, *that text cannot be fulfilled*, because we can no longer, in this world, identify anyone by their place of origin. The Talmud, in the third century, says, *mi'she'ala sancherev u'bilbel et kol ha'u'mot*. At a particular moment in time—it marks that moment in time as the Assyrian kingdom—you can no longer identify a person by their place of origin, so none of the texts from the ancient world that suggest that you can attack a person based on their racial source are valid. They are all nullified. That was the fundamental position of the Talmud: nullifying any text that would allow for distinction in moral treatment based on racial origin.

Christianity has tragic texts in the book of John, which were used by Goebbels in World War Two—Goebbels, the minister of propaganda for Nazism. And Christianity has evolved and said "No" to those texts, and rejected those texts, and stood for a wider and more beautiful and deeper world. Christianity has gone through a profound evolution. Yes, there are shadow forms of Christianity, and there are shadow forms of Christian theology, and there are dimensions of Judaism that still need to be evolved and transformed. But both Christianity and Judaism have, at the very core of their establishments, gone through an experience of what I would call the evolution of consciousness and the evolution of love, which caused texts to be challenged and up-leveled and evolved and transformed in a very fundamental way.

In other words, **Judaism and Christianity interpenetrated their experiences of waking up to an experience of the Divine with an experience of growing up to higher and higher levels of consciousness**, so that they began to reject certain texts. The current Pope, for example, has made a very strong position of moving towards a deep evolution in the transformation of consciousness—long overdue in the Catholic Church, maybe a thousand years overdue or more.

Tragically, the most dominant forces in international *realpolitik* that root themselves in Islam, and Islam in general, have not gone through that same interpenetration with values of universal sisterhood, universal brotherhood, the emergence of the feminine, and the dignity of the body, universal human rights. That hasn't happened. The experience of Islam interpenetrating with an enlightenment, a Renaissance, with the values that emerged from the Renaissance, the positive values of universal sisterhood and universal brotherhood—that actually didn't happen.

When Sam Harris pointed this out in his own forum (and I read maybe one article that he wrote about it, a long time ago), he got brutally attacked by the emergent woke communities. But he was right, it's correct.

THIS IS NOT A STORY OF MORAL EQUIVALENCE

I read *The Boston Globe* at about 5am this morning. It describes what happened as a morally equivalent battle between the Hamas fighters and the Israeli soldiers, and then it describes how the Hamas fighters went and rampaged through Israeli communities, including a nature festival in the south of Israel. Let me be clear: Hamas fighters were not *rampaging* through Israel. *Rampaging* means breaking windows and roughing people up a little bit. No, that's not what they were doing.

The tragically educated and horrifically twisted culture of Hamas, which basically views people outside of *Dar-al-Islam*, the nation of the Islam, as those to be subjected to destruction by the sword, entered a nature festival with thousands of Israeli kids, teenagers, and massacred them. They massacred hundreds of kids—butchered and massacred. They didn't *rampage*. They sought the most vulnerable civilian populations and massacred them, and then they went into houses and massacred families: men, women, children. That has been part of the fundamental methodology of Hamas. They didn't rampage. **This is not a story of moral equivalence.**

I am deeply, deeply aware of the complexity of the Middle East. I lived in Israel for many, many years. I lived in a home in Jaffa, in Arab Jaffa, with an Arab family, with great love and delight. I've taken major stands in Israel about how we need to work, and coexist, and share, and create a shared sense of value with our brothers and sisters. That's all true. But if you follow and trace this story carefully, if you get beneath the news, if you read real grounding documents and trace the storyline of how this has developed, which I can't do in this short presentation, you will understand the following.

Israel is—with all of its complexity, with all of its tragedy, with all of its imperfections, of which it has many—a thriving democracy based on a sense of universal human rights. Hadassah Hospital, at the center of Jerusalem, which is grounded in the ethics of Israeli democracy, serves every Jew and Arab who enters, with Jewish and Arab doctors working side by side. There was a reason it was nominated for a Nobel Peace Prize. There is tragically no other capital in the Middle East other than Israeli Jerusalem that would allow for the existence of a Hadassah Hospital, where anyone, regardless of race, could go in and know that they would be treated fairly, and beautifully, and gorgeously, with devotion.

That would not happen in any Arab capital, anyplace in the Middle East, and certainly, there would be zero chance of that taking place any place within the province and realm of Hamas. Let's just understand that. The Hamas-Iran nexus, whose overt covenant is dedicated to the annihilation of Israel, would never allow for a Hadassah Hospital—but Israel does. **The failure to distinguish between these different structures and levels of consciousness is utterly destructive.**

I must have read, this morning, five or six accounts in different mainstream outlets of the Western press. I see things like *Hamas fighters rampaged in an Israeli festival*. They didn't *rampage* in an Israeli festival, they *massacred* hundreds of high school students. Those are not the same.

If we trace the history of the story—and I have spent thousands of hours tracing the history of how the story began and developed over the last 100-150 years—what's very, very clear is the following.

The overwhelming majority of the Israeli population has been willing, time and again, to make peace and to share the space and to share the land, in some appropriate way.

There are twenty-one or twenty-two Arab states with vast amounts of lands and reserves. There is one tiny Jewish state. That Jewish state itself has been willing to make a thousand compromises for the sake of peace, and there has not been an ethical, stable partner for peace on the other side.

That's simply true. That's an undeniable fact. And if you contest that fact, you actually have not traced the story. Again: there have to be facts. There's got to be some ground of fact.

If you read, for example, the code of ethics of the Israeli army, prepared by Professor Asa Kasher and others in Israel, you will read one of the most profoundly, shockingly gorgeous ethical documents ever written in human history. That's the aspiration of the Israeli army. When someone violates that, they are court-martialed, they are sent to prison. Yes, the system breaks down at times, yes there are aberrations; there are always aberrations. But those aberrations are the exception to a very strong rule, which the overwhelming, overwhelming majority of the Israeli population holds.

By contrast, tragically, on a street controlled by Hamas (in Gaza, for example), when someone sees an Israeli car and sees children in the backseat, they shoot into the car—at the children, at the parents—and kill them. This has happened time and again, time and again, and has happened to people in my family. It happened to me, driving a car with my child in the backseat, although I managed to get out at that particular time. That's standard practice: to become a murderer. That person becomes not an outcast, but a hero.

This is *not* because Israel has a powerful army, and there is this weak and disempowered population, and the only method they have of political discourse is terrorism. For Hamas, that's not the case. **The reason this situation exists is because Hamas has incarnated an utter rejection of the fundamental values of universal human rights, the fundamental values of universal fairness, the fundamental values of the honor of the feminine, the fundamental values of fact-checking and truth**—and the list goes on and on and on and on and on.

The ideology of Hamas is based on that rejection, on the distortion of Eros, which expresses itself in a distorted love story, a tragically distorted love story, in which love means—not even love of my people, but much worse

74

than that: "I love only my people who adhere to a very particular and narrow interpretation of the law of the prophet."

That narrow interpretation of the law of the prophet has to include utter commitment to the annihilation of the State of Israel—this is in the very core charter of Hamas. If you don't adhere to that, or if you assert, for example, the independent integrity and autonomy of the feminine, independent of its service to the masculine, you're in violation of the law of the prophet.

For example, honor killing—killing a woman who is suspected of having "fooled around" with someone—is completely legitimate, and no evidence needs to be brought that the woman was actually in violation of this ostensible moral turpitude. One merely says one was engaged in honor killing. Check it out, there is an enormous amount of information and an enormous amount of empirical data gathered on how honor killings happen.

Or if a man, in the world of Hamas, has proclivities towards being gay, he is killed. There was a major Hamas leader killed a bunch of years ago for being gay, killed in a brutal, horrific, torturing way. Hamas represents the cruelties, the shadow of a medieval world, in its most brutal forms.

We can't skip this my friends, we can't skip this. We can't go to moral equivalence. I know this is going to be, for some people, an unpopular position. But if we can't actually stand for a shared grammar of value, then the whole thing collapses.

THE DECONSTRUCTION OF VALUE AROUSES HAMAS

We need to create a universal culture of Eros. A culture of Eros means a culture of value. In this new Story of Value we're committed to unfolding a series of *interior science equations* which express a shared grammar of value. Among them, as the first equation, we articulate *an Eros equation*:

Eros = the experience of radical aliveness, desiring, seeking ever deeper contact and ever greater wholeness.

We are talking about *Eros as a value of Cosmos*. It means deeper contact: between parts, between life forms, between separate parts seeking to create deep and profound, intimate communions.

That's the structure of Cosmos that begins all the way down the evolutionary chain and goes all the way up the evolutionary chain, to create larger wholes, in which all the parts have a place, in which no one is outside of the circle. That Eros is a value of Cosmos. It's not that there's Eros *and* value—there is *ErosValue*; a Field of *ErosValue*.

This Field of *ErosValue* is a structure of Reality, and it demands something from us. It demands our devotion. It demands our sincerity. It demands our generosity. It demands our gratitude. It demands our service. It demands the pouring of our unique gifts into the healing and transformation of the whole. It demands a relationship to the whole. It demands the realization that we are unique expressions of goodness, truth, and beauty.

Each of us has a unique instrument to play in this larger Unique Self Symphony. But this Unique Self Symphony, in which we are all playing our Unique Self instruments, is held together, grounded, in a shared score of music. That music is the ground of value. It's the ground of Eros. It's the Intimate Universe.

If we don't embrace that, and instead we articulate a *deconstruction* of value, if we say—as one of my colleagues does—that there is no value, that all values are the same, that there is no difference between medieval value in which Christians go to the Holy Land to kill Muslims, and contemporary democracy—as one well-known proponent of postmodern discourse argues. If you make that argument—if you say, *There is no Field of Value*, or *All value is completely made-up*—in that deconstruction and denial of the Field of Value, you *arouse* Hamas. Because Hamas—as a phenomenology in the world, as a force in the world—listens in and says, *Oh my God, the*

West has just deconstructed and denied value itself. There is no value. There is nothing to sacrifice for. There is nothing to stand for. There is nothing with which we need to align. There is nothing before which we need to kneel. There is nothing that elicits our devotion. There is no larger frame. There is no larger story. There is no Reality that demands our service."

When that claim is made—a false claim, an absurd claim, a claim which empties Reality of significance, Eros, and value—**it leaves a gaping wound, a gaping gash in the very heart of Cosmos**. In that emptiness, in that collapse of Eros, in that failure of Eros, in that failure of a story of Eros Value, what arises is *pseudo-eros*: false love stories, narrow ethnocentric love stories that brutalize and degrade the other. But what fuels those pseudo-erotic love stories is a desperate desire to affirm value, and so value is affirmed as: "*My people, my Allah, my Christ, my tribe."*

AT THE CORE OF THE HAMAS NARRATIVE IS A DEGRADATION OF DESIRE

There are two other pieces at play. **One is *shame*. This pseudo-erotic love story, where love is limited to a very small group of people**—so everyone outside of that group is not worthy of love, is not to be loved, is not to be honored, can be degraded and dehumanized, because everyone outside of that circle of love is considered to be not fully human, and therefore can be slaughtered at a nature festival, without regard, with intention—**that story is rooted in this fundamental shame.**

This is so deep, and it's so tragic, and it needs to be understood. That shame is rooted in a degradation of the experience of desire and love itself. When you tell a person, *When you murder someone outside of this narrow circle, that's not murder—that's for the sake of the Lord, for the sake of Allah.* That person's interior sense of the mystery, that person's interior sense of goodness, truth, and beauty, that person's interior sense of the realness and goodness of Cosmos that lives in us, are violated.

Do you think you can paraglide from Gaza into Israel into a nature festival and slaughter dozens of teenage women, and *not* experience a profound revulsion and shame about who you are?

Do you understand the shame caused by your participation in that kind of slaughter, in that kind of destruction of love, or that kind of limitation of love: *I love only this small group, no one else is worthy of love*—not only *they're not worthy of love,* but *they're worthy of the worst degradation*—it's the shame of your own interior degradation.

But there is a deeper root shame, and the deeper root shame is that *your very desire itself has been degraded.* In other words, in Hamas' vision of Reality, the story of desire is that desire itself is fundamentally degraded, that sensual desire is fundamentally degraded, that the sense of goodness and truth and beauty that lives in the body is fundamentally degraded.

This was also the story of the Catholic Church till very, very recently, but it reigns in Hamas today, and it reigns in Iran today. This is why Mahsa Amini and hundreds of Iranian women were tortured and killed in the last year, including high school girls.

You degrade desire, and yet that desire continues to live and to *rage*—in the young men of Hamas, and the young men of the Ayatollah Revolutionary Guard, and the young men of the military wings of Hamas and Hezbollah.

And so, the self-experience of these young men is: "We are *degraded*, we are fundamentally *impure*, we are fundamentally *revolting* to the Divine, we are somehow *disgusting* to the Divine."

There is this internal sense of shame, and an inability to trust the core experience of the body. And when there is an inability to trust the core experience of the body, when there is a fundamental degradation of desire that lives in a human being, then the human being becomes alienated from their own capacity to trust themselves and to trust their moral sense—to use an outdated eighteenth-century term—then **the human being becomes alienated from their own capacity to trust their deepest participation in**

the Field of *Eros Value*. All of that gets alienated, gets truncated, from a person's inner heart. The person no longer has access to the whisperings of goodness, truth, and beauty that live within them. That's huge.

At the core of the Hamas narrative, there is a degradation of desire. That degradation of desire causes fundamental shame.

Shame means the experience not that I did something wrong, but that I am wrong.

That experience that *I am wrong* is so fundamentally painful, that we can't live with it, so we cover it up. We cover it up with pseudo-eros, which are fantasies, in which *"Love lives in this very narrow place between me and my very internal narrow set of people, and everyone else outside of my circle is an infidel, to be butchered and killed for the sake of some illusory fantasy of purity."* It's like, wow!

WE NEED TO ARTICULATE A NEW GROUND OF DESIRE

Shame gives rise to this pseudo-erotic fantasy of purity: shame at my own murderousness and failure of love that arouses hatred to anyone outside of my circle, shame at the ostensibly degraded desire that lives in my body— because desire itself is degraded.

All of that shame alienates me from any sense of my ability to participate in the Field of Value, and to know the goodness and truth and beauty that lives in me, and to be guided by that goodness, truth, and beauty.

This creates an unbearable pain inside of me that needs to be covered over by pseudo-eros. Read Hamas' covenant and you'll see pseudo-eros aflame in all of its most horrific disguises.

But again, what gives rise to that is the claim that *there is no value*. When the classical liberal position of the Western world says, *There's no value at all, there is no Field of Value*, our response to that is: *There is value*. But value can get expressed in its most distorted forms.

When there is no consecration of value—when there is no altar at which we kneel, when there is no service that we are called towards, when there is no sense of a higher obligation and a higher responsibility, when there is no sense of devotion, or sincerity, or generosity, or ethos, when none of those exist as intrinsic features of Cosmos that invite us, that honor us, by demanding our participation and dignifying our capacity to participate, when there is a field devoid of Eros and value—then pseudo-eros rears its head in the most horrific ways.

In other words, **when you destroy a healthy experience of my whole self—** of my sanctified self, of my holy self, of the holy Eros that lives in me— **then you create an experience that is so fundamentally painful for the personal and the collective, that you get every form of breakdown**—every form of fascism, every form of Khomeini-ism, every form of regressive, degraded expression of hatred, which come together as organized forms of pseudo-eros.

When there is no holy Eros, there is only pseudo-eros. This means that the only way to respond to this degradation is by articulating a new Story of Value which is Real.

This is a new Story of Value which evolves through us, which we incarnate in our very being, and is also the mystery before which we bow, before which we are in service, before which we are in devotion. **If we can't articulate a new Story of ErosValue, a new Story of Desire, then it all breaks down.**

The core point of the movie *Barbie* is that there is no love story in Cosmos. It is quite explicit in the movie that any notion of value is made up. Human meanings are made up. We live one life, we die, it's over, and any meaning we had along the way we simply made up.

That's the position that Hamas is reading. That's what Hamas is understanding as being the bedrock of what they call the West—and they are not entirely wrong.

That's a big deal. Hamas responds by an utter degradation of *Barbie* in an extreme horrific expression of patriarchy at its worst, through the role of the masculine in Hamas' ideology. That's actually what happens. But what is the response in Western culture? The response is the *Barbie* movie, a universe in which *there is no love story*, and in which *everything is just a social construction*.

But then a second expression of that universe becomes a pornographic universe, in which desire is digitally mediated and you have a complete overwhelming of the senses, deluged by images of incarnate desire which are dissociated from larger fields of divinity and larger fields of dignity.

I've had so many men walk through my office in different ways, and talk about growing up on high-speed internet porn from age nine or ten, with no sense of a narrative of desire—of Reality that is desire, of Reality that is a Field of Desire, of the unique desire and unique script of desire that lives in me, as me, and through me. None of that's available.

We need to articulate a new ground of desire, a new Story of Desire. **To be *Homo amor* is to be able to live and incarnate that new Story of Desire.**

PURITY OF DESIRE

Hamas views its goal as *purity*. There is this great yearning for purity. But actually, the place you can access purity is in the purity of Eros, or in the purity of the sexual, or the purity of Fuck. But the purity of Fuck is not available through the pornographic universe.

The pornographic universe is simply an unclarified desire. It's simply laziness. It's the allowing of artificial intelligence to hijack my unique script of desire. The purity of Fuck is actually difficult to get to:

A place where you are beyond shame, and you are experiencing the Fuck of Reality, the great kiss of Reality, the current of the Eros of Reality moving uniquely through you, in all of its purity.

When you pour that energy that moves through you into Reality itself. When giving and receiving become one. When respect abounds, and every play of desire is burst with open heart and open *LoveDesire*. That's the purity effect. That's a hard one. That's unavailable to Hamas, and it's not available to the postmodern West.

The new story is saying "No" to the pornographic universe, and "No" to the regressive world of fundamentalist degradations of desire. **It's a new vision, in which Fuck itself is not opposed to purity, but in its clarified form, in its deepest clarified experience of desire, you access an unimaginable purity**—which is why people may have that experience maybe once in their life. Sometimes people can access that experience by doing a medicine journey, and then mixing that medicine journey with embodiment. But it *is* actually available. **Once you have that experience, you realize that purity lives inside of you.**

In the experience of Hamas, there is no experience of the purity of desire.

In 325 CE, in the original council that formed the Christian church, there was an argument about "Who is Christ? Is Christ *of* God or is Christ *like* a God?" It is based on how you read one particular Greek word.[2]

Now, what's the difference? Well, if Christ is *of* God, then Christ is unique and singular: "It's only Christ, no one else, only Christ is of God. Only Christ is Christed. Only Christ is Divine."

---

2 Homoousios.

But if Christ is a human being who is *like* God, it means that Christ goes through a transformation to become like God—just like Enoch, in the wisdom literature, is originally a human figure, who is then transformed into Metatron, into the Godself. In other words, is the Christ figure every human being who can be transformed, and *"I can be transformed because I can embody the Christ in me?"*

An embodied Christed experience of sex is love in the body. And I can experience the purity of desire in me.

What Hamas has said is: *"No, it's only God. It's not you. You can't have purity of desire in you. Your desire will lead you astray. You cannot trust your body. There's nothing that you can trust internally."* Therefore, the only possibility of Reality is radical authoritarianism—and of the most degrading kind.

SHOCKS OF EXISTENCE PRESS US INTO GNOSIS AND NEW EMERGENCE

We have been talking, since 2011 or 2012, about the meta-crisis and the second shock of existence. The first shock of existence is the experience of the human being: *I'm going to die at the end of this life.* There is an experience of death. That experience of death forces me into myself, *presses me to the wall*, to use Rilke's words. When death presses me to the wall, I have a much deeper realization of who I am, and what value is, and perhaps I may actually generate a realization of a continuity of consciousness beyond death. Death presses me into life. Death presses me into gnosis.

In the original experience of the first shock of existence, we are pressed against the wall of existence, if you will. We go deep inside, and we begin to generate *knowing:* knowing of value, knowing of goodness, knowing of truth.

We begin to generate fields of meaning. It takes thousands of years for those fields to evolve.

It's the encounter with death that pushes us into the realization of value.

In our deep analysis of the movie *Don't Look Up*, we studied this realization of death, when finally people realize existential risk. A meteor in this movie is going to hit the planet, and there is this last scene where the heroic figures in the movie all gather and they have dinner together in the last minutes of reality. And they realize: *What matters is eating together, and loving each other, and saying grace together, and clasping hands, and giving each other a hug, and opening our hearts and loving.* All of a sudden, in the face of death, you realize: *Oh my God, this is what value is!*

My son wrote in a family text thread last night: *All I want to do is to be at home with my three kids, I want to be at home; nothing else matters, I just want to be at home with my family.*

I am not saying that's the only value. That's one set of values. It's a beautiful value. When I encounter death—personally, myself—I am desperate to love. And one of the ways I am desperate to love is to write this Great Library at this time between worlds, and download it into Reality, and to stand for this new Great Library and this new Story of Value, and to pour every ounce of my energy and effort into making sure that we can articulate this new Story of Value and drop it into Reality, download it into the source code of Cosmos as a gift for thousands of years to come.

That original experience of the death of the human being pressed us into gnosis, and it also moved us to create families. In a family there is a father and a daughter, and a father doesn't take advantage of his daughter sexually; she is not a sexual object. The father protects the daughter.

There is this emergence of the father, the couple, the family, the clan, the lineage, the perpetuation of family, the wider family that gathers and holds each other—these all emerged from the first shock of existence.

In the first shock of existence, one of the things we did was we looked at sexuality and we said, *Wow, there is this wild force in Cosmos called sexuality.*

And we tried to create containers to hold it, which were all forms of ritual, and all forms of guidance, and all forms of categorization: *This is fallen sexuality, this is sacred sexuality.*

Some of it we got right, and a lot of it we got wrong, but there was this attempt to create containers to hold the erotic, to hold sexuality.

We now come to the second shock of existence. The second shock of existence is the potential death of humanity.

Just like the first shock of existence pressed us into new knowing—new gnosis, new forms of family, new forms of the sexual, new visions of meaning—now the second shock of existence also has to press us into new emergent value: new stories of desire, new visions of a sexual ethos, new visions of the erotic and the ethical.

We need to come not to a place where we deny value, not to a place where we deconstruct all value.

We need to be once again pressed against the wall of Reality into disclosing new visions of meaning, which means new sexual ethics, a new ethos, new visions of what *Eros* means.

A NEW CULTURE OF EROS: THE DEMOCRATIZATION OF HIEROS GAMOS

In the ancient world, virtually all sexuality was in some sense diminished in its sacred character, and the only true sacred sexuality was often that of the king and the queen, or the priest and the priestess who engaged in *hieros gamos:* in sexual coupling for the sake of the people.

All other sexuality didn't have that status. Only the sexuality of the king and the queen, or of the priest and the priestess, had ultimate value. Often, they would engage sexually in a temple ritual for the sake of the people, and then be put to death as a sexual sacrifice. That was the *hieros gamos*, the divine marriage in the ancient world, in which there was this realization that the power of the sexual needed to be harnessed—but it was harnessed in a way in which it resulted in an actual physical death, and it was reserved for the elite.

We are now at this new moment in which the old ethnocentric world of *it's just about my people* and *we love only my people* doesn't work. We face global challenges, and we need a global grammar of value. And we realize that it's not about just the king and the queen; that every human being is royalty, and there is a sense of universal human rights, and there is the emergence of the feminine. **We need to claim what we might call the democratization of *hieros gamos*. We need to reclaim the sexual current of desire that lives through us.**

Not the script mediated by the pornographic universe. Not the script of my desire that was stolen from me and imposed upon me by the most reductive forms of a broken capitalism. Not the script that robs ten-year-olds (who become fifteen and twenty-year-olds) of their ability to access and arouse their own unique fields of desire. Not that.

We need to liberate ourselves from the tyranny of a pornographic universe that erases our scripts of desire, and reclaim our own sexuality.

---

*I need to reclaim myself as the priest
and priestess, reclaim myself as the
king and queen and move towards a
democratization of hieros gamos.*

In other words, the second shock of existence presses us into a new narrative of sexuality, a new narrative of desire. It's not that sexuality is *sex-negative*, or it's not just bland *sex-positive*. And it's not—like for Kinsey, the sex researcher—*sex-neutral*: "it's just like having lunch." And it's not *sex-sacred*: "because it creates babies." No.

- It's a democratized realization that sexual desire is the nature of Reality.
- It's the realization that the name of God is desire, and that desire is the currency of Reality.
- It's the realization that Reality is *ErosDesire*, and that *ErosDesire* lives uniquely in me.
- It's the realization that in my sexuality is—that I am—a unique incarnation and expression of the entire Field of Desire.

It's the realization that because I feel sexual desire moving in me—which is desire for pleasure and fullness, and the goodness of life, and the desire to give and share that with someone—**I am actually a priest and priestess of the new Reality.** I am a citizen of this new global world, and my sexuality is sacred and needs to be protected and honored.

I need to distinguish between fallen sexuality and sacred sexuality. I need to access my deepest heart's desire. I need to access my own unique script of desire.

We need to reclaim a new narrative of desire, which is our response to shame. Shame is when there is a degradation of desire and that desire lives in me, then it makes me feel abhorrent to myself. But when I honor the dignity of desire, and I realize that desire lives uniquely in me, I realize that my sexuality—with myself if I live by myself, or with another—*is* the divine marriage. It's me marrying all the parts to myself, or me in relationship to another.

Sexuality is so sacred that anyone that I've even felt sexual arousal towards, I need to be in devotion to my entire life. Of course, I don't need to *act* on any of that sexual arousal, I can be classically monogamous my entire life. Yet I can honor my entire field of desire, and honor *everyone's* field of desire, and realize that everyone is a king and queen, a priest and priestess, engaged in a unique *hieros gamos*, and that the bed of sexuality is the bed of ethics and the bed of value, and that value lives in the sexual experience (as the sexual is a model of Eros).

Why does value live in the sexual experience? Because it's about devotion, and it's about giving, and it's about giving and receiving being one.

We need to reclaim the experience of the sexual as a model of Eros, as the most sacred dimension of life. That's a solid alternative to the degraded visions of a pornographic universe. That's a sexuality that we stand for, that we live for, that we die for: when we realize that our own tumescence, and our own throbbing, and our own pulsing is the pulsing of God and Goddess. Do you begin to see this vision?

All of that—the entire culture of Eros we just described—is absent. It doesn't exist anyplace. In that absence you get pseudo-eros and in that absence you get degraded visions of desire. Hamas is built on a degraded vision of desire and a degraded vision of the feminine, so of course it slaughters teenage boys and girls in the field, because it's filled with its own shame.

But of course, the Western liberal world has failed to create a powerful compelling vision—a grammar of value to which we are in devotion, which is deeply articulated, which is felt. We worship on the altars of our own narrow narcissisms. We need to create new altars, to create new visions of value.

THE BATTLE BETWEEN GOOD AND EVIL EXISTS IN EVERY HUMAN BEING

The other dimension that mixes in with the degraded worldviews that are expressed in Iran today, and in Hamas, and in Hezbollah is what we might call the Ring of Sauron—to borrow Tolkien's imagery from *Lord of the Rings*. The Ring of Sauron is actually the dark, degraded ontologies of evil that live in the world.

The lack of Eros creates pseudo-eros.

When there is no genuine Eros, there is pseudo-eros: there are all forms of acting out, all forms of addiction, and all sorts of power drives that seek to cover over the emptiness of genuine Eros.

Those pseudo-erotic power drives have enormous power. They are fueled by a pseudo-erotic ontology of evil. In other words, evil is not just the absence of good; evil develops its own appetites, its own hungers. The hungry ghosts of Buddhism have a kind of ontology, they have a kind of power. And, of course, that was depicted in Western literature as the devil. But while the devil is absurd in its grotesque and caricatured depictions, what's not absurd is that there actually *is* a battle between good and evil in the world. That battle between good and evil exists in every human being. There is a battle between the part of me that wants to be gorgeous and stunning, and the part of me that wants to be contracted.

Just find the moment when you are in a fight with someone, and they accuse you of doing something wrong, and you don't want to acknowledge that you might have done something wrong, even if you did. You want to lash out and destroy them because you feel ashamed. So what do you do? Do you respond from your fullest self and say: *Wow, you just pointed out that I did something wrong! Wow, let me just look at it. Oh wow, there's something to that, my bad, I apologize. Oh wow, I really own that, thank you. Oh, and now let me share something else*—and then go on to the next part of the conversation? Or are you triggered in shame and lash out to destroy the person? This is that battle between good and evil.

Can I reach deep in myself and find my joy? Can I find my love? Can I find my generosity? Can I show up when it's impossible to show up? Can I be in devotion when I don't want to be devoted? Can I be fierce when I need to be fierce? Can I be fearless standing for the Field of Value, even when it's not comfortable politically and I may lose some egoic standing in the world? Can I be aligned with value?

That battle between good and evil exists in every person. It exists in every community. It exists between people. There *is* a battle for good and evil in the world. Sorry, it's true. No, it's not the old mythic version of the battle, with the good Christians against the bad Jews, or the good Muslims against the bad Christians, or the early versions of the Bible 3,500 years ago, which is the good Jews who are doing their thing, who are going to destroy Canaan (which the Hebrew wisdom tradition said is not valid).

No, we've got to evolve beyond that.

We totally need to evolve beyond that, absolutely, beyond the old mythic versions, where it's very easy to say, *I'm on the side of the good and you're on the side of evil*. It's very easy to get caught in the battle of good and evil and make myself the good and everyone else the evil, and demonize the other and not see them at all.

We get that, so we need to reject *that* notion of the battle between good and evil—but **there *is* a battle between good and evil, that's actually**

true. There are two kinds of forces that exist and live in the world. Tolkien wasn't wrong when he talked about the Ring of Sauron and the nine kings seduced by the Ring.

PSEUDO-EROS EXPONENTIALIZED BECOMES THE RING OF SAURON

And what is the Ring? The Ring is a circle, and a circle is always a symbol of circle Eros, and the circle Eros is a particular kind of depth in Reality. The nature of a circle is that it's not trying to get somewhere, it's *for its own sake*. It's called *lishma: for its own sake*. The circle is *for its own sake*. In its beautiful vision: "I want to sit and have a conversation with you *for its own sake*, my son wants to be with his family *for its own sake*, we want to love each other *for its own sake*." That's beautiful.

But there's a shadow of *for its own sake*. And the shadow of *for its own sake* is the desire for *power-over* for its own sake. The desire to assert my power by inflicting pain on the other for its own sake. The desire to avoid shame by asserting my superiority through utter degrading or murder of the other.

The shadow of *for its own sake* is towards the destruction of the other:

- I create a circle, and everyone else is outside of the circle.
- I create pseudo-eros.
- I am on the inside because everyone else is outside.

I am driven by this seductive drive for power, the Ring of Sauron, and power becomes the value itself. In other words, pseudo-eros exponentialized becomes the Ring of Sauron. And the Ring of Sauron is called *precious*. Remember the hobbit who becomes evil in the Tolkien trilogy of *Lord of the Rings*, he talks about the Ring and he says, *my precious, my precious*. What does *precious* mean? Value. The point is, the Ring becomes "value"—but it's really anti-value. **It's the pure raw drive for power which overrides**

all value. There is no sense of Eros. There is no sense of real devotion. There is no sense of kindness.

Do you remember the orcs? The orcs are the manufactured brigades of "fighters," who go out to fight for Sauron, who massacre everything in their way. Those orcs have no kindness. And they have no sexuality, no sexuality that's beautiful. They are lost in pornographies of violence. Those are the orcs.

There is a battle between good and evil. But it's not between individuals of different racial origin. It's not "good Jews and bad Arabs," or "good Christians and bad Jews." It's not "good Chinese and bad Americans." **It is never about racial origin. It is about the system of value in which we live.**

What is the Grammar of Value in which we live?

What is the Story of Value in which we live?

There is no child born into a Hamas family that cannot grow up to be a gorgeous good, true, and beautiful, noble human being—a noble knight of goodness, truth, and beauty. There is nothing intrinsically broken or fallen about Jews or Arabs or Christians or Yellow or Brown or Black or Red. Of course not. It's about *What is the Story of Value?*

Am I engaged in the evolution of consciousness and the evolution of love?

Am I evolving value?

Am I accessing my deepest heart's desire?

Am I trusting my capacity to be a responsible agent and player motivated by my deepest heart's desire?

Or have I demonized my interior desire, so I cannot trust my desire, and therefore I am controlled by a Story of Value which is built on the degradation, destruction, and the murder of the other?

Friends, there is a battle between good and evil, and we do need to take a stand in that battle.

And it's not all *realpolitik*, and it's not all corrupt, and it's not true that "*it's just corruption all around.*" **Yes, there is corruption in every system, and there is no system that's not without its deep flaws. But there *is* better and worse, and there *are* higher and more degraded forms of value.**

And there is—I want to say it again—there is a battle between good and evil. That's real, and we need to take our stand in that battle. It's not a moral equivalence all around. There is no moral equivalence between the Russian army and the Ukrainian army. I am familiar, very deeply familiar with all the flaws and complexities that are happening in Ukraine. I am aware of that. And at the same time there is no moral equivalence between what the Russian army is doing and what the Ukrainian army is doing, even though they are both flawed in many ways. But there is a very clear need and value to support Ukraine in the best way possible. That's true, with all the complexity. And it's clearly true in Israel.

GREATER IS THE LIGHT THAT COMES *FROM* THE DARKNESS

I'm going to end how I began: with the Hadassah Hospital, and pluralism at the very center of the society. It is this tiny little country which has the most advanced code of ethics for its army. It's an aspirational code that the army strives and stretches to live by. Even now in the middle of the horror, warnings were given in Gaza whenever possible to evacuate places where the army was going to operate. The whole thing is imperfect. The whole thing is a holy and broken *Hallelujah*.

- ◆ But there is a battle between good and evil.

93

- And we can trust our deepest heart's desire, which incarnates our moral compass.
- We do need to be telling a new Story of Desire and a new Story of Value.
- We need to be madly committed to that story, and we need to stake our lives on it.
- We need to be willing to bracket our narcissistic selves for the sake of the larger whole. That's what arouses the respect of Reality itself. Wow!

We cannot have Hamas hijack God. The god of Hamas is a distorted and degraded god, which is idolatrous, which serves, tragically, the degraded forms of the great impulse of goodness that is the spark that's at the heart of every great system of value, of every great system of religion, of *re-ligare*—reconnecting. But as Abraham Kook writes, when you degrade your vision of God, you degrade your vision of ethos, and very quickly, you become a mass murderer.

There is a great battle between good and evil, and our role in that battle here is: we are going to give everything we have, with every breath we have—not as a casual side activity, not as a hobby as we go through our narcissistic lives—**we are going to lay it all down to tell a new Story of Value.**

Not just to tell it, not just to declare it. We are committed to writing, with depth, a Great Library, and to grounding it in the deepest sciences, and the deepest footnotes, and the deepest universal grammars of value, liberating the deepest sparks from every great tradition, and creating the ground of a world religion as a context for our diversity: where there is a place for a gorgeous holy Islam, a gorgeous holy Judaism, a gorgeous holy Buddhism, gorgeous holy Sunnis and Shiites. The tragedy of Islam is that within Islam, murder reigns between every faction. No. Let's have a shared value within Islam, a shared Christ Field.

We are committed to this. We are going to do everything we can to articulate in every language we can, this new grammar of value, and to validate it. Not just to *claim* it, but to *validate* it. That's not a two-year project; that's our life's work. We are going to publish it, and write it, and film it, and share it in every way we can. That's our fight. We are fighting. We are in the great battle of good and evil.

And lastly, we have to own the shadow in us. The only way to be in the battle of good and evil is to know that it's not just binary. Any evil that exists out there also in some place lurks in my heart—and so I have to find that inside of me and transform it. We say in the text of Solomon: "Greater is light than darkness." And then the masters say, in the thirteenth century, not "greater is light than darkness," but rather "greater is light that comes *from* the darkness." We have to own our own shadows. We have to own our own flaws. We have to own our own vulnerabilities.

Not with a sense of moral equivalence; we are all flawed and vulnerable, but there are distinctions, and these are important distinctions.

Yet we never make evil solely the place where *the other* lives. We always look deeply. We are willing to be displeasing to ourselves. Because it's only by being displeasing to ourselves that we can be at an altar to the Divine: at an altar to the Christ, at an altar to the true Allah, at an altar to the true Atman that is Brahman, at an altar to the true Adonai Elohim.

Amen, amen.

CHAPTER SIX

BARBIE, HAMAS, AND HOMO AMOR: FROM DEGRADED LOVE STORIES TO THE UNIVERSE: A LOVE STORY

Episode 369 — November 5, 2023

RESPONDING TO THE CULTURE OF DEATH AS *HOMO AMOR*

We need to clear our glasses. We need to be able to see clearly. *Homo amor* needs to be able to clear glasses, to clarify the interior, to be able to stand in love, to be able to stand in Eros.

If you've tracked and understood the fabric of interior culture, the confusion is not surprising. But sometimes something can be not just surprising, but shocking.

The confusion undermines the capacity to be *Homo amor*:

- The incapacity to distinguish between the utter tragedy of innocent civilians being killed in Gaza—or anyplace in the world, which rips our hearts out—and the jihadi culture of death.
- The incapacity to distinguish between a culture of *death* and a culture of *life* (which may have thousand problems, but is fundamentally a culture of life).

We need to be able to make these distinctions.

The first requirement of *Homo amor* is that we feel the joy. We feel the joy, the pulsing joy of the world, and when there is pain, we feel the pulsing pain of the world.

No one's blood is cheap. Ukrainian blood is not cheap, and Yemenite blood is not cheap, and Jewish blood is not cheap, and Palestinian blood is not cheap. All blood has the same value, the same intrinsic value. No one's blood is cheap.

***And* we need to be able to make the fundamental distinction between a jihadi culture of death, and at least an aspiring culture of life that needs to respond to it.**

In order to be able to respond to the culture of death we have to first understand it, and then we need to embrace a new Story of Value. From where we stand today, we don't have the capacity to respond to the culture of death as *Homo amor*.

I'm going to try and be as precise as I can today and outline *Barbie* (the movie), Hamas, and the new story. These are the three options we have for the world today.

1. Barbie, as we'll see, will lead to a nihilistic destruction.
2. Hamas will lead to a puritanical destruction.
3. Only a new Story of Value—which realizes with mad joy that the universe is a love story, that I participate in that love story, that no one is outside the circle—can respond and move us from horror to hope.

That realization is based not simply on *declaration*, but on a careful reading of both the hard, exterior sciences and what I would call *the interior sciences*, the wisdom traditions. **It's only such a realization**—it's only such an evolution of culture and consciousness, it's only such a progression of moral grasp and understanding, it's only such a progression of *ethos* rooted in a realization of Eros—**that can respond to the culture of death and create the new world, the more beautiful world that our hearts know is possible.**[3]

THE REFUSAL TO MAKE DISTINCTIONS CONTRAVENES THE INTERIOR OF *HOMO AMOR*

Love is not merely a feeling—I haven't stopped feeling. I feel insanely. I am by nature an empath, so I feel all the time; I'm always feeling. I have never, quite literally never, had a good idea in my life. Any idea, any Dharma, any set of distinctions that I am trying to articulate comes from a deep feeling, a felt sense, and I try to articulate the feeling as it stays with me. Day in and day out, I try to articulate the feeling and then share it. I am trying to share a *feeling* and then to articulate it in a *distinction*. We have to feel.

But it's only our capacity to feel *and articulate* this new Story of Value that can allow us to move from horror to hope, to the *hope which is a memory of the future.*

FALSE STORIES CONFUSE US

Stories *matter.* Story is the very structure of Reality itself. Story is not a human invention; Story is ontological to Cosmos.

In the interior sciences, there is a phrase we sometimes use: *God loves stories.* That's another way of talking about story as structural to Reality.

Don't worry if you're confused about God. As we often say, the god you don't believe in doesn't exist, it's okay. The god that you deny, I deny also. **When we talk about God, we mean the Field of Value which is infinitely personal.**

In CosmoErotic Humanism, we have a name that we use to refer to the Divine that both *lives in us* and *holds us,* and that name is the *Infinite*

---

3 To quote our friend Charles Eisenstein.

Intimate. God is the *Infinite Intimate*: the Infinite that desires intimacy and becomes somehow paradoxically *more* infinite through desiring intimacy and through realizing ever deeper intimacies.

Why does that matter so insanely much in this very moment? This is because false stories confuse us.

I'll give you an example of a false story.

The atrocity of October 7th took place because of the interior logic of Hamas, which is a failed love story. It has nothing to do with the occupation, whatever *the occupation* means. That word doesn't even *mean* anything, it's an overused trope, "the occupation of Gaza." Who is occupying Gaza, what does it even mean? Where is Gaza? When was it part of Egypt?

Israel unilaterally withdrew from Gaza. Hamas took it over, threw out Fatah, and basically massacres and kills its citizens at will in order to hold them captive for its own jihadi aims. Whenever someone says *the occupation of Gaza*, they don't know what they are referring to and have no sense of the storyline.

I'll give you a better piece of evidence. If you study the history of the Islamic State, ISIS, in Iraq and in Syria, there was no occupation there—no West Bank, no Israel, no Jews, no occupation—and still, the Islamic State acted with barbarity and cruelty and atrocity of the same nature.

Or if you see the movie, *Hotel Mumbai*, which is about another jihadi set of atrocities which killed some 160 people. Again, there is no Israel there, and no occupation, and no Zionist entity—none of those smokescreens. And jihad does what jihad does. That's really critical to understand.

It is very clear that Hamas, although quite distinct from ISIS, is operating in the fundamental logic of a culture of death.

We're going to go much deeper than that. That's just the very beginning. But clearly, that's not about an occupation. First, because the word *occupation* doesn't make sense in the Gaza context.

Secondly, how do you know the difference between a reason and an excuse? If you remove the excuse, does the phenomenon still exist? That's a very good distinction. If the reason for Hamas' atrocities is a response to a political agenda posed by Israel, well, then remove Israel, remove Jews, remove any of those factors, and will jihadism still carry out its atrocities? The answer is, yes. Whatever the political sets of issues are in Gaza or the West Bank, they are not the cause. (By the way, based on all the polls today, Hamas would win an election in the West Bank; let's just hold that).

Someone just wrote in the chat box: *This is not jihad, it's pseudo-jihad.* **The most important thing that could happen in the world today would be that the interpretation of jihad as an internal struggle for liberation would be accepted.** That would be the most beautiful, gorgeous evolution. That has not happened. We need two billion Muslims to arise in the world and say, *what jihad means is internal transformation.* Amen, Hallelujah! That is what needs to happen.

We need an evolution of consciousness within Islam.

However, if you read the classical interpretations that are dominating the discourse, jihad is *very centrally* about violence and war, with Muhammad as the model. That is their interpretation of jihad that they're now enacting. We need an evolution of what jihad means, and that would be probably one of the most pivotal evolutions of consciousness that we could enact.

A FAILED LOVE STORY ON A COLLECTIVE LEVEL RESULTS IN HORROR

But let's go deeper. Hamas is not a group of sociopaths. It's critical to understand, Hamas are not sociopaths. They're not psychopaths. There might be a random sociopath and psychopath, and there may be more than a few, like there always is. If Hamas was just basically a group of mafia sociopaths, we would have a much smaller problem.

No, the whole point is that **Hamas are ordinary people who are fundamentally psychologically sound, who have been completely absorbed in a failed love story.** The acts they carry out are an expression of an utterly distorted version of a love story. It's an utter degradation of a love story. That's the point.

We heard a recording of this young man Muhammad, who calls home and he says, *I killed ten Jews, and I just killed this woman, and I have her phone and I'm calling you with her phone, and I'm sending images of the Jews that I just killed with my own hands to my WhatsApp.* And his father says, *you killed ten Jews?* And his mother is there crying, but there is a shared conversation between them.

Compare this to the My Lai massacre, Lieutenant Calley and the My Lai massacre and Medina, I think it was Sergeant Medina, in Vietnam. Can you imagine Calley and Medina calling home to Wyoming and Nebraska and telling their parents, *Wow, I just killed ten people?* The parents would be horrified. *You're out of your mind! What the fuck happened to you?* That's not what happens in this phone call. There is a culture of jihad.

And the father says, *When are you going to come home?*

His son replies, *Martyrdom. Victory or martyrdom.*

Clearly, martyrdom was where Muhammad was going. Muhammad is not evil in the sense that he's expressing a psychopathy, he is not. He is not a psychopath. He is not a sociopath. He is a normal person with some elemental psychological soundness trapped in a failed love story, and this is far, far more dangerous. Just ask O.J. Simpson what it means to be trapped in a failed love story.

A failed love story on a personal level is O.J. Simpson, which results in murder. But a failed love story on a collective level results in horror. In the fourteenth century, it resulted in the horrors of the Crusades: burning heretics alive and flaying their skin. And in the jihadist moment, it results in this ultimate violation of *Homo amor*, and the unimaginable atrocities of October 7th.

That's just our context. And the context is, *story matters*. The story you tell matters.

LET'S GET OUT OF SUPERFICIAL DISTORTIONS

We are trying to step out of the horror of social media feeds. They are so often utterly lost in the sad dimensions of human beings. Their architecture and their incentive structures are perverse, and all too often reward the lowest common denominator of human expression. Let's get out of social media feeds.

Let's get out of this unimaginably superficial set of distortions, colored by any number of motivations, of the kind that existed in so much of the legacy press.

For example, some time ago, when a hospital was bombed, and Hamas immediately said, *Israel did this*, and Israel said, *well, of course not. The New York Times* and BBC and *Reuters* and *The Guardian* all reported, based on Hamas, that Israel did it, without any checks or verification. **And it turned out, based on all the available intelligence in multiple vectors, not to be true.**

What caused our legacy press institutions to do that is a deeper conversation that we're not going to have now.

Let's get out of those vectors, both out of the legacy press and out of the social media feeds, and let's look clearly, with our hearts wide open.

Our intention is to come to joy.

Our intention is the evolution of love.

Our intention is to clean our glasses, to see clearly.

EVOLUTIONARY LOVE CODE: *HOMO AMOR*, THE ALTERNATIVE TO POSTMODERN MATERIALISM OR PSEUDO-EROTIC VIOLENT FUNDAMENTALISM

There are three Universe Stories:

1. The *Barbie* Universe Story
2. The Fundamentalist Universe Story
3. And then there is the *Homo amor*, CosmoErotic Humanism Story, the new Story of Value

Those are the three choices that we have today. It's not a binary choice; we need to find a third way. We need to find our way between the binary of *Barbie* and Hamas (Fundamentalism) —between postmodern, desiccated, empty materialism and a pseudo-erotic fundamentalism, which is wildly destructive. The third way is the new Story of Value rooted in evolving First Principles and First Values: CosmoErotic Humanism.

UNIVERSE STORY 1—*BARBIE:* "THERE IS NO LOVE STORY"

The movie that played in theaters in lots of the United States just as the Hamas atrocities were happening was *Barbie*. This is culture telling a story. This is the Intimate Universe whispering. What is *Barbie* saying? What is the *Barbie* story about? If you follow the movie carefully, Barbie is not saying here, *I'm not in love with this Ken.* This is not a personal Barbie and a personal Ken. Barbie and Ken here are archetypes. They are two parts in a larger system, and the question is, *is there a love story in the system or isn't there?*

The entire plot of *Barbie* is that there is no love story.

That's why Barbie says to Ken, when he moves to kiss her in the beginning, *what are you doing?* And he says, *well, maybe I'll stay over.* She says, *why would you stay over? It's girls' night, every night, forever*—meaning: forever, eternity is not about eternal love. Eternity is not about a love story. There is no love story.

If you carefully read the lyrics of the key songs in the movie, "Closer to Fine" and "I'm Just Ken," the point of the songs is: "there *is* no love story." *Barbie is not in love with Ken* means Barbie is not in love with Ken, period. Love is *not* the end of the story. It's not where we're going. It is not just a healthy individuation, which is how we would *like* to understand Barbie: Ken has to individuate, and Barbie has to individuate, and then they come together in this new Eros and this larger love. That's exactly *not* what Barbie is saying, if you read the text carefully. Barbie is saying, there is no love story.

There is an incredible scene where Barbie is talking to Ruth, Mrs. Mattel, the founder of Mattel. Barbie says, *I want to become a human.* And Mrs. Mattel, Ruth says, *why?* And Mrs. Mattel describes human beings and says, *and in the end, they die.* Death, that's the end, it's over. They just make up meaning along the way, they just basically make shit up, because the whole thing is this fleeting thing, and why would you want to join that? No answer to that question is given in Barbie.

It is very, very different from that moment in Tolkien, in *The Lord of the Rings* trilogy. Arwyn, who is an eternal—or close to eternal—elf, decides she wants to become human even if she loses her eternity, in order to be with Aragorn. She wants to be with Aragorn because **Reality is a love story, and because love is an eternal value of Reality itself**, so to step into love is to step into eternity.

That's precisely *not* what's happening in *Barbie. Barbie* is a world in which death ends life, in which after death, there is only nothingness. There is no Field of Value. "*Humans make it up, it's not real.*" Therefore the closest that *Barbie* can get to a love story is biological, so the relationship between Sasha and her mother is a love story. There are about five or six scenes where that biological love story unfolds. Even Ruth says, *I named Barbie after my daughter, Barbara.* It's the mother-daughter story, the feminine

104

biological love story, because the masculine is demonized in Barbie. That's as close as we can get to a love story, but the core is there is no love story. That's *Barbie's* point. **There is no love story because love itself is not a value, because Eros itself is not an intrinsic value of Cosmos.**

You have a postmodern desiccation—as Lewis Mumford called it, a *disqualification of the universe*. There is no Field of Value, and there is no ultimate distinction between right and wrong. That distinction can't be drawn. It's an arbitrary distinction.

As Yuval Harari basically says, "*there is no difference at all, in any ultimate sense, between massacring Muslims in the fourteenth century as a Christian young knight, and going to that same region of the world to work to heal refugees for Amnesty International.*" He says quite explicitly, "*Those are both just made-up stories, and in a few hundred years, the story we tell now, the Amnesty International story, the positive Western value story, will also seem absurd to us. There is no ultimate distinction.*"

I'm not citing Harari as a thinker. He's not important as a thinker. He's important as an "uncontaminated" source—in the sense of being an unconscious parrot of the zeitgeist—as reflected in *Barbie*—which is that "*there is no love story.*"

CLARIFIED DESIRE DISCLOSES VALUE; EROS IS A VALUE OF COSMOS

When there is no love story, all you get is the drive for power. All you get is rivalrous conflict governed by win/lose metrics. What you get is a war machine. You get a military industrial complex, you get a medical industrial complex. You get the lowest common denominator of human drives, which are drives of *pseudo-eros*.

Eros is not just Eros. Eros is the movement of separate parts desiring deeper contact and greater wholeness. Eros is the experience of radical aliveness.

This is the new Universe Story.

In the new Universe Story, desire is real; it is a value of Cosmos. When you clarify desire, your clarified desire tells you what you value. Desire is an appropriate and legitimate and important compass. **I follow my clarified compass of desire in order to disclose value.**

IF THERE IS NO EROS, THERE IS PSEUDO-EROS

Eros is a value of Cosmos. But if there is no Eros, then there is only emptiness. We try to fill it up, because we can't bear the emptiness. Postmodern materialism has no explanation of *why* we can't bear the emptiness. **Existentialists like Sartre and Camus describe with great grotesque detail the experience of emptiness, but they ignore the question of *why* the emptiness is there.** Why do we feel this emptiness, if we are but desiccated, flatland, postmodern, mechanical humans without any intrinsic value? They can't explain that.

If there is no Eros, there is pseudo-eros. Pseudo-eros appears in many forms. One form of pseudo-eros is a military industrial complex—this flexing of muscle, this drive to war, the war machine. Postmodernity can produce war machines, and war machines benefit from wars. Whenever there is a war, you'll always have to try and see: *Where is the hidden war machine?*

Postmodernity creates a moral vacuum. Moral vacuums benefit war machines that traffic in raw power. We all just have to be aware: *Is there a war machine someplace here, someplace in the background?* And feel where it is. Not all war machines are the same, and there are wars that *need* to be fought, as I've talked about, as the Dalai Lama has talked about. Pacifism is not an option, if I am taking responsibility for love, and for the present, and for the future.

What emerges out of the *Barbie* dogmatic claim—that there is no love story because there is no Field of Value, and therefore no *ErosValue* in Cosmos—**is pseudo-eros that goes to destroy everything, through its rivalrous conflict governed by win/lose metrics.**

That's one story. In this story, desire is not a value of Cosmos. Desire is not sacred:

> I can't listen to my desire. My clarified desire means nothing. It is just the social construction that dominates who I am. There is no free choice. There is no choosing of direction. It's an illusion. It's made-up. My experience of freedom is dismissed because my experience is dismissed. And my desire for freedom is dismissed because desire has no ontology. It has no reality. It has no ultimate moral force.

That's the first story. So what is *Barbie*? A failed love story. A failed story of desire.

What is Hamas? In a completely different way, it's the same interior structure.

UNIVERSE STORY 2—HAMAS: THE DEMONIZATION OF DESIRE

Obviously, there is *zero* moral equivalence between *Barbie* and Hamas. But in terms of its interior structure, Hamas is also a failed love story: There is no universal grammar of value rooted in Eros. There is no universal Field of Eros.

In this story, Reality is divided in only one way. It's not divided between regions, or geographies, or nations, certainly not nation-states. It is divided in one way, *Dar Al Harb* and *Dar Al Islam*: those who should be brutally subjugated, and those who are purified by the only pure version of Islam. Whether it's the Sunni version or the Shia version of jihad is a deadly argument between those versions of jihad—but what they share is that *only a purified Islam is worthy of care and concern and love.* **In this failed love story, the body is demonized.**

The stirrings of desire in the body are demonized. Masturbation has no place. Self-pleasuring has no place. The joy of making love, within the right and sacred context, has no place.

That's critical: the body cannot be trusted. The stirrings of desire in the body can't be trusted. Rather, martyrdom—the rejection of the embodied manifest reality—is at the center of the conversation.

Now, if the body cannot be trusted, and I experience, deep in my body, the stirring of desire—which is in violation of the purified version of Islam which has animated my consciousness from early childhood—then I feel there is evil in me. **I cannot *own* that evil, so I project it outwards**—on *the other*, on the enemy, on the infidel, who needs to be slaughtered by the sword, and painfully.

Anthony Blinken, the Secretary of State of the United States reports—this is a firsthand testimony from Gaza—about families being tied together, children and parents, with the limbs of the children, fingers and legs, cut off. We're talking about phalluses of men cut off before their raped women, and then everyone burned alive.

This is what we're talking about. We're talking about this most torturous, most brutal, most vicious slaughter, to inflict the most pain possible. To cut a girl's arm off and leave her, without killing her, intentionally, so she'll wallow for seven hours in her pain. That's the intention.

Then she quivers and dies in the end, as one of the first responders arrives hours later. **Because the experience of desire has been degraded, because desire is not holy.**

POSTMODERNISM AND FUNDAMENTALISM ARE BOTH FAILED LOVE STORIES

Barbie, in its way, *disqualifies* desire. In this narrative, desire is not real, desire doesn't tell me anything real about Reality. ErosDesire—desire which is the face of Eros—doesn't lead me to ethos.

In the Hamas version, desire is not just disqualified, but degraded and demonized, and therefore the body can be violated. An anti-desire *torture*—the opposite of desire—is inflicted in the name of this purity. **The**

experience of interior desire, which is experienced as evil, is projected outwards, and then that desire is killed, and destroyed, and violated.

That is the interior logic of the jihadi position. Not because they're sociopaths, not because they're psychopaths, but because that's what the good martyr does, inherently.

That's why even though the details of all these killings were known, they were *celebrated*. The atrocities were celebrated on two different streets: They were celebrated on the postmodern street, in universities across the world, including the best of Western liberal universities, who live in a postmodern predicament in which there is no Field of Value.

When there is no Field of Value, you cannot do *evaluation*. If there's no Field of Value, you cannot evaluate anything. Evaluation makes distinction. We lose that capacity, which is where moral equivalence has come from.

And they were celebrated on the street in which jihad is celebrated. Even if one is not an active jihadi, there is an enormous sympathy to jihad throughout huge swaths of reality. There is this demonized degraded desire, which allows for an embrace of this jihadi worldview, which is then celebrated in huge rallies around the world.

UNIVERSE STORY 3—THE REALIZATION THAT THE UNIVERSE IS A LOVE STORY

A third possibility is a return to Eros. But it is *not* a return—it is the articulation, for the first time, of the *realization* that the Universe is a love story.

We've said many, many times that existential risk is *global:* climate change, artificial intelligence, the gap between haves and have-nots. Global challenges require global solutions. Global solutions require global coordination. Global coordination requires global resonance, or global coherence. We need global coherence in order to resonate with each other in order to coordinate. Global coherence requires global intimacy. Global intimacy—like intimacy in any relationship—requires a shared story of value.

But there is no shared Story of Value. There is a degraded fundamentalist value, and there is a desiccated, disqualified value of postmodernism. **Barbie and Hamas, both swelling movements in the world**—postmodernity and fundamentalism—**are both failed love stories; they don't have a shared Story of Value.**

Only a shared Story of Value can respond to existential risk, which is the death of humanity or the death of our humanity.

A disqualified value produces the military industrial complex, and it also produces TechnoFeudalism—a technocratic totalitarianism, a structure designed to undermine free will, and to undermine choice, and to appeal to the lowest common denominator of human beings. And then you've got the fundamentalist position with its demonization of desire, and all of its utter horror.

So what's the response? The response has to be a third way. And the third way, the third possibility, this new allurement, is the realization that:

- The Universe is a love story.
- Eros is the ground of Reality. Reality is Eros.
- Eros is the value of Reality.
- Reality seeks value. Reality has an appetite for value.
- Reality is *DesireEros* and intimacy seeking ever deeper uniqueness, ever deeper diversity, and then ever larger unions from that diversity, and ever deeper goodness, truth, and beauty.

That's why failed love stories are so dangerous.

THE UNIVERSE: A LOVE STORY

Look at a four-letter name of God:

ה ו ה י

Hei   Vav   Hei   Yud

Going from right to left:

- The *Yud* enters the *Hei*. Together they make the sound *Yah*, as in Leonard Cohen's *Hallelu-yah*. The breath of Reality is the *Yud* entering the *Hei* in mad Eros.
- And then the *Vav* enters the *Hei*, the third letter enters the fourth letter, again, in mad Eros.

In the interior sciences the *Yud* entering the *Hei* is called the *constant* Eros of Cosmos: electromagnetism, gravitational allurement, the strong and weak nuclear forces, the structure of Reality.

And the *Vav* entering the *Hei* is called the *aroused* Eros of Cosmos. The aroused Eros is the Eros generated by that same quality of allurement and desire, but now operating at the depths of human self-reflective consciousness.

In the interior sciences, Reality is *Names of God*, which is just another way of saying: Reality is allurement. Reality is Eros. Reality is desire. And desire means: I am seeking value, I am desiring ever greater value. Reality has *an appetite*—"appetition," in Whitehead's words—for value.

That's a love story. **The Universe is a Love Story.**

> *The Universe is animated by desire. So I can trust my desire, and my desire tells me truth. I can trust my body.*

Do you feel that? The book of Job—as it's read by the interior sciences—says, in Chapter 19: *Through my body, I vision God.* Meaning, *I can trust my body.*

The stirrings of desire in my body—not in their pseudo-erotic form, not in their addictive form, not in their broken form, but my *clarified* desire—**discloses value.**

- It is my desire for creativity.
- It is my desire for caring.
- It is my desire for nurturing.
- It is my desire for responsibility.
- It is my desire for aliveness.
- It is my desire for union.
- It is my desire for ever deeper intimacies, for ever deeper truth-telling, for ever deeper transformation, for ever deeper uniqueness.

These are the First Principles and First Values of Cosmos, which are the First *Desires* of Cosmos.

The First Desires of Cosmos are its First Values, and the whole thing is a love story.

This is why one text says: *Histakel b'oraita*: She (the *Shekinah*) looked in the text—and the text is the names of God—*u'bara alma*: and the world is an expression of the names of God. Meaning: Reality is desire. God is Eros, all the way up and all the way down.

We are unique participatory expressions of the Field of Eros: Unique Selves, unique incarnations of intimacy and desire.

That's a love story. And *ethos* comes from that love story.

THE MORAL IMPERATIVE OF THE UNIVERSE: A LOVE STORY

When there is no love story, when Eros is not a value, you have emptiness and you have pseudo-eros. Whether it's the postmodern version of pseudo-eros, or the fundamentalist version of pseudo-eros, they both produce destruction. Our response has to be the overriding moral imperative of this time—as it was for da Vinci and Ficino at the Florentine Platonic Academy in the Renaissance, which was also a time between worlds and a time between stories.

In this moment, in this breach, we have to not just *tell*, not just *declare*, but *articulate, research, deepen, write, clarify* the evolution of the human story, which is that:

- Reality is a love story. Love is a value of Cosmos.
- No one is outside of the love story.
- We all participate in that story. We all have unique contributions to that love story.
- That love story is evolving, it is clarifying all the time.

That's *the Universe: A Love Story.*

That love story has got to be so powerful, and so pulsing, and so throbbing that it awakens Barbie and Ken, that a Hamas apostate, the person who leaves Hamas, doesn't become a postmodernist—which is what's happening

113

now. Those who leave Hamas, they go to Europe and become postmodern apostates, because the choice is either Hamas or postmodernism. No.

We have to *initiate* Reality—as da Vinci and Ficino did—**into this new love story, grounded in the best of the sciences**. That's where we're going. That's what we are here to do.

Is it *Barbie* or Hamas?

No, it's *the Universe: A Love Story*.

CHAPTER SEVEN

EROS AND GNOSIS AND ETHICS ARE ONE: REALITY IS EVOLVING CODES OF DESIRE

Episode 371 — November 19, 2023

THE BREAKDOWN OF SENSEMAKING

There is no question in my heart, mind, body that there is a "before October 7th" world and there is an "after October 7th" world. October 7th was the moment when the primary enemy of the Palestinian people, a degraded version of fundamentalism—Hamas—brutalized and tortured the feminine. Raping seven-year-old girls and cutting off their arms in front of their mothers—just to get a sense of what we mean, so we don't turn away from it.

The enemies of the Palestinian people, Hamas, who are holding the best of Palestinian aspirations hostage, performed acts of butchery.

But that's *not* why October 7th is a watershed moment.

Tragically, there has been butchery in the world before:

- ◆ Unimaginable tragedy in Iran—the killing of girls by the Iranian regime, pulling girls out of high school (and of course, Iran is backing Hamas).
- ◆ Horrors on the battlefield in Ukraine, and Putin's attempt to destroy Ukraine.
- ◆ Child soldiers in Yemen, Sudan, Congo.

All of this is taking place in a larger context of a world that's filled with Beauty, and filled with Goodness, and filled with Eros, and filled with wonder, and filled with delight. It's all happening at the same time.

But the reason that it's a "before October 7th" and an "after October 7th" is because **the utter incapacity to do sensemaking was radically exposed in an unimaginable way**.

It was an utter breakdown of the sensemaking apparatus.

When the Holocaust happened in Europe, it took *decades* for people to have the temerity to deny that it happened. After October 7th, we were experiencing denials *within a couple of days*. In the last week, the denials have picked up steam. And now the formal position of an unimaginable amount of people on various forms of social media is that these atrocities didn't actually happen.

The enormous amount of first-person and second-person eyewitness testimony and digital evidence are essentially dismissed. Denial is happening within a few weeks. **There is also an inability to *discern*, to follow *a storyline*, to make *distinctions*—not a primitive taking of sides, but discerning a hierarchy of value**. There is a deafening silence of major Western universities all over Europe and the United States. The reporting of BBC and some of the French news outlets is so shockingly in violation of elementary sensemaking that it's almost unimaginable.

I am not going to talk about Israel today, and I am not going to talk about Hamas today. I am not going to go into ten examples of where and why. I just want to feel it with you.

There is this breakdown in sensemaking, in the ability to make sense, in basic capacities to know, to make simple distinctions.

THE FUTURE OF REALITY DEPENDS ON OUR CAPACITY TO ARTICULATE A SHARED STORY OF VALUE

I want to talk today about how we *know*, about how we *make distinctions*, about how we do *sensemaking*. Because that's everything.

The breakdown of sensemaking is but one expression of an utter breakdown in any kind of *shared story of value* in the world. And there is absolutely no question in my body, heart, mind that **the future of Reality depends on our capacity to articulate a shared Story of Value**, in which everyone is at the table. China is at the table, and Russia is at the table, and the United States is at the table, and Islamic fundamentalism finds its way to the table, and postmodern disqualifications of Reality find their way to the table.

We need a new Story of Value grounded in the nature of Cosmos itself. **We need a cosmic, galactic Story of Value, which is** (to borrow the word from Aramaic and French) **"un-fuckwithable"**—meaning it is so *grounded*. It's so *well-done*.

It's not declared. It's not dogmatic. It's not fanciful. It's not conjecture. **It's the deepest voice of She.**

EVOLUTIONARY LOVE CODE: THE SENSUALITY OF SENSEMAKING

A wise man once said:

When we feel, we can begin to think.

And only then can we begin to engage in the sensuality of sensemaking.

Love and knowledge are not separate.

Eros and gnosis are not separate.

What we think is less than what we know.

117

What we know is less than what we love.

What we love is so much less than what there is.

And to that precise extent, we are in practice so much less than what we are in reality. [4]

To be what we are, truly, we need to love.

We only know what we love.

We only love what we know.

When we know, we can begin to feel.

WHAT WE THINK IS LESS THAN WHAT WE KNOW

What we think is less than what we know. *What we think*—that's my cognitive mind, but it's much smaller than what I know. What is *knowing*? What does it mean, *to know*?

What we're going to try and look for here is *the common sense* of Reality. Declared dogmas are almost always strategies for the hijacking of power—dominator forms of power, not sacred forms of power—and they need to be rejected.

But underneath declared dogmas, there is a *common sense*.

Now, what does *common sense* mean? Common sense means that there is a common field of sense between us. *Sense* is *sensual*. **Sense means that underneath the superficialities and the vagaries of surface thinking, there is a deeper big mind**—*Daishin*. A deeper big heart, big mind.

There is a bigger *mochin de-gadlut*, in the Aramaic tradition: expanded heart-mind consciousness, which we all share.

There is a common sense. **Our common sense is the beginning of our common sensemaking.**

---

9 Referring to a quote from R.D. Laing.

GLOBAL RESONANCE REQUIRES A COMMON SENSE

We live in this time between worlds and this time between stories. In the space in between, there is a meta-crisis. The meta-crisis operates in about fifteen vectors: from artificial intelligence to methane gas under the tundra. Israel-Hamas is just one expression of that meta-crisis.

In order to respond to the meta-crisis, we need global coordination. We can't have global coordination without global coherence. We can't have global coherence without global resonance. **We have to *resonate* with each other, which means we need *common sense*. We need common *sensuality*. Common sense creates a sense of *intimacy* between us.**

When we don't have this shared intimacy and shared sensuality, we don't have that shared resonance, we can't create coherence and we can't coordinate—and the meta-crisis quite literally destroys us. The incapacity for common sense creates a global intimacy disorder. It can only be healed through common sense, which is a shared Story of Value.

To sum up:

1. In order to respond to this meta-crisis, we need common sense.
2. Common sense means a shared story.
3. A shared story has to be a shared Story of Value. A global intimacy disorder means there is no shared Story of Value.
4. But it has to be value that is grounded in Cosmos—not contrived values, not dogmatic values, not values claimed by the Shambhala masters or the Hebrew masters.

This is value that the greatest masters incarnated in their bodies, hearts, and minds, in a democratization of sensuality that we can all access directly.

We can directly and clearly access this value in our bodies.

THE SHARED STORY OF REALITY IS THE STORY OF REALITY'S SENSUALITY

- The shared Story of Value is the structure of Reality.
- The shared Story of Value is the sensuality of Reality in the narrative form.
- The shared story of Reality is the story of Reality's *sense*—the sensemaking of Reality, or the story of Reality's sensuality.

You can't split *sensemaking* from *sensuality*. Reality is a story, and we live in that story. That story is both sensible and sensual. At its core, it is a story of desire. **A shared story of value is a shared story of desire.** My code of value is my code of desire.

We are used to thinking of sacred texts as codes of *value*. But underneath, **sacred texts**—at their best, at their very core—**are codes of *desire*.**

We said sensemaking and sensuality are deeply related. Let's just follow that *in language*. *To love* is *to know*. To love God is to know God. For example, when Maimonides and Aquinas and the medieval scholars talk about loving God, whatever that means, they directly link *loving* God and *knowing* God. **There is no split between love and knowledge.** I love what I know, and I know what I love. There is a virtuous circle that moves between love and knowledge. If I don't love you, I don't know you. And if I don't know you, I don't love you.

In Hebrew, the word *yada* means "to know," as in, "and Adam *knew* his wife Eve." Knowing is carnal. We call it in English, *carnal knowledge. He knew her biblically* is a phrase in English. I don't know what the Russian or Italian or French or Dutch equivalent is, but *to know* is *to know carnally*. All knowledge is carnal knowledge—or, said differently: **There is no essential split between Eros and gnosis.**

Eros—sensuality, the field of the sensual—is the place where I do sensemaking. It is the matrix of common sense. It's the common field of the sensual, from which no one is excluded. Everyone is in the circle of the sensual. It is a *common* sense.

It is only common sense—or common sensuality, or common Eros—that can yield a common gnosis, a common knowing. That knowing becomes a new Story of Value, a new grammar of value.

This is so because Eros encodes itself in story. That's the nature of Reality. Eros is always Eros in action. Evolution is love in action. Evolution is Eros in action, seeking, desiring evermore Eros, evermore sensuality. Reality is Eros. That's what Reality is.

EROS IS A DYNAMIC CREATIVE MOVEMENT OF REALITY

Eros means something very, very particular. Eros is a story. It's a movement of Reality. It's not *static*, it's *dynamic*. Eros is this deep ground of *being—* being at home, this essential *being-ness* of Cosmos: "*I am at home, I am grounded, I am welcome in Reality. Ah, I can rest.*" And then, Eros is movement, it's a *becoming.*

Eros is the spaciousness of Being, and Eros is the ecstatic urgency of becoming.

What is Eros? Eros is the experience of radical aliveness, desiring ever deeper contact, ever deeper touch, and ever deeper wholeness—so that from that touch, from that contact, a new emergent, a new possibility, a new wholeness is generated. That is Eros. That's the structure of Reality.

The interior experience of Eros is this desire for ever deeper contact and ever greater possibility, which is ever greater wholeness. When we come together as separate parts and form a new whole, that wholeness creates a new possibility. Sometimes that possibility is a baby. Sometimes that possibility is a manuscript. Sometimes that possibility is a new emergence, a new force. Sometimes that possibility is a *Phenomenology of Eros*.

When we come together, we create. Eros is creative by its nature.

All men and women are born equal. All men and women are born erotically creative.

THE CODE OF DESIRE OF REALITY IS WRITTEN IN THE EROS AND INTIMACY EQUATIONS

Eros is desire. Now, this desire for deeper contact, and for greater wholeness, and for greater possibility, is really a desire for *intimacy*. I want intimacy. Because what is intimacy?

Here is the intimacy equation:

Intimacy = shared identity in the context of [relative] otherness, plus mutuality of recognition, mutuality of feeling, mutuality of value, and mutuality of purpose.

1. Intimacy means a new shared identity between the parts. Two people come together. They were living separate lives and all of a sudden they began to experience themselves as part of a larger whole, a new wholeness, which can have many forms. That's a new intimacy.
2. There's a new shared identity in the context of otherness: *I don't disappear. You don't disappear.* It's not *fusion*, it's a *union*.
3. We recognize each other (mutuality of recognition).
4. We feel each other (mutuality of feeling).
5. We have a shared Field of Value (mutuality of value).
6. We have a deep sense of a shared purpose (mutuality of purpose).

Here is the Eros equation:

Eros = the experience of radical aliveness, seeking, moving towards, desiring, ever deeper contact and ever greater wholeness.

The code of desire of Reality is written in the Eros equation and intimacy equation. The Eros equation and the intimacy equation are codes of desire.

TWO CODES OF DESIRE: CODE OF REALITY AND SACRED TEXTS

The first code of desire is the Code of Reality Itself. The sacred texts of the great traditions are later codes of desire. They're commenting on—and they have to *emerge from* and be aligned with—the Code of Desire of Reality itself.

Now, let me just say clearly:

You cannot have ever greater wholeness if your heart doesn't break for every innocent person killed in Gaza.

You can't have greater wholeness if you're in an ethnocentric position—if you want to perpetuate your egoic ethnocentric entity for its own sake—independent of the Code of Reality. An ethnocentric code of desire that views the other as outside the circle of Eros is a code of desire that violates Reality. It's a false code of desire. It's a *pornographic* code of desire. Shadow versions of ethnocentric consciousness, which are *othering* those that are outside of their ethnocentric circle, are pornographic.

REALITY IS *EROSVALUE*

Reality is a Field of Eros, or a Field of Desire. This Field of Desire desires—what? Ever more intimacy. So, the story of evolution is:

1. Evolution is Eros.
2. Evolution is Eros in *action.*
3. What is the action of Eros? *Desire.*
4. What does Eros desire? Value. Eros desires value. Or, said differently, Eros *is* value. Eros is the desire for value, and value itself is Eros.

What does Eros desire? Eros desires more wholeness, more contact, more shared identity, more mutuality of recognition, more mutuality of feeling, more mutuality of value, more mutuality of purpose.

Eros is the core value of Cosmos. That's what Eros is—Eros desiring Eros, which is more intimacy, which is more desire, which is more mutuality of desire, and more mutuality of feeling, and more mutuality of recognition, more contact, which generates more wholeness (equals more shared identities). Do you begin to feel the loop? It's so deep. It's so beautiful.

Reality is ErosValue. And ErosValue itself is the LoveIntelligence of Reality.

The word *love* itself is a desiccated word, which has lost its meaning. We tried to have the word *love* stand independently of all words, and we thought it would survive. We killed all the goddesses except for Aphrodite. But then we realized we didn't know how to worship at Her altar. Because you can't kill all the gods, meaning, you can't kill the Field of Value and then just leave love standing by itself. **Love is Eros. Eros is a value of Cosmos.** That's what it is. That's its very nature.

What is Eros? It is *ethos*. It is *value*. There's no split between them.

Eros is the desire for deeper contact, and *deeper contact* means contact that *honors*, that has mutualities of recognition and mutualities of feeling and mutualities of purpose and mutualities of value. It's intimate contact that generates new emergence. It means it generates greater wholeness. It's not just even that Eros *speaks* value. Eros *is* value. You cannot split the words Eros and value. It's not that Eros *is* a value. It's that Eros *is* value, and value is infused and flamed with Eros. *It's Eros Value.*

HOW DO YOU KNOW VALUE IS EROTIC? BECAUSE VALUE AROUSES OUR WILL

How do you know value is erotic? Because value arouses our will. We are *moved* by value.

We are in the middle of Covid, and the entire liberal community is in the classical vaccine narrative, and everyone believes that to leave our houses could endanger millions of people. And then George Floyd is killed, and the entire liberal community spills into the street to protest for George Floyd. And they should have, and that was good, and I joined the protests. Those are good protests.

But why? Because we were aroused by the violation of value, which aroused our will. Eros arouses our will, we throw everything else to the side, because that's what we do when our will is aroused.

Will is *ratzon*. *Ratzon* comes from the Song of Solomon in Chapter 1, Verse 3 and 4, "Seduce me." *Na-rutzah.* "I will run after you." *I will run* is *rutz*, which also means *ratzon*, which means my will is aroused. My higher will, my essential will is aroused, and I throw to the wayside everything which is ancillary, everything which is superficial, everything which is exterior.

When I cross a certain moment in sacred sensuality, and am now all the way inside, I am in the experience of value, I am in the experience of Eros. There is no difference between them.

125

Mashcheni Acharecha, "Draw me after you"—that's the beginnings of coming together in Eros. Then you cross that line, *na-rutzah*, "Now I'm running towards you." When I am with the right person, in the right place, in the right context, I don't stop and ask, "Is there value in the world?" No, *this is* value. Eros and value are one.

Value is erotic. Value arouses my will. It aroused our will to protest for George Floyd. Value arouses our moral will. Value arouses our political will. Value arouses our economic will. It's *only* value that is arousing. That's critical to understand.

By the way, this is something that TechnoFeudalists, who want to create a techno-totalitarian world in order to protect humanity against existential risk, don't understand. They think value is not real. And *"Because value is not real, you have to control the whole world. You cannot let anyone know you're controlling them, or they'll rebel. Give them an illusion of freedom. Put everyone in a Skinner box"*—a box in which you pull the levers on the web, and undermine people's free will, and control the masses of humanity.

They do it not because they're evil. I reject the demonization of techno-totalitarians that appears all over the web. That might be part of the story, but it's far from *all* of the story. All of the story is: they feel that value is not real: *Since value is not real, it's not arousing. We can't appeal to a new Story of Value, we can only control.*

THE EXPERIENCE OF VALUE LIVES WITHIN THE EXPERIENCE OF EROS

Eros means contact, deep contact between us. I'm kissing my beloved's shoulder, we're holding hands, just that simple moment of contact. Because Eros and sensuality is not some sort of caricatured penetration of a particular kind. It's contact of the heart, contact of the body, contact of the mind.

126

Desire means I desire to make contact. When I make contact—let's take the sensual image of the Song of Solomon—it's that moment in which I've crossed the line. I am on the inside. I don't ask, "Is value real?" I don't have to make anyone realize value is real. I realize it directly in my body in this moment. I don't stop and say, "What's the value of the world?" I don't stop and say, "What's the meaning of life?"

When I am in those two minutes before the ecstatic explosion, and I'm all the way on the inside, you've drawn me after you—in the language of the text of the Song of Solomon—now I'm running towards you. Stay with me. I'm running towards you.

Just find that. Stay in that. Don't let your mind wander. Stay in that. Find that one time in your life when you were on the inside, when you crossed the line, and stay inside of it. Stay inside of it. *That one time in my life where I was on the inside, I had crossed that line in sensuality, and I was moving towards expression, towards fulfillment. I was on the inside. That was value.* Don't let your mind wander. That's a lazy mind. Stay centered.

That's the experience of value right there. *I know it in my body. I know that that's valuable.* That experience of intrinsic value lives in the experience of Eros.

Eros is value, and value is filled with Eros. There is no split between them. They are one.

Because, again, what's the Eros equation? Eros equals the experience of radical aliveness, desiring ever deeper contact.

I am desiring ever deeper contact. I am coming closer, closer.

I am desiring greater wholeness, which means I am desiring more intimacy. We are going to come together—we are not going to disappear, we are not going to fuse, but—there is going to be the sense of shared identity in the depth of our conversation, in the depth of our lovemaking. And the depth of our lovemaking might be me kissing your shoulder, it might be the depth of our eyes locked in each other.

Oh my God! That's it, right there. That's it. *That* is value. That is the experience of value right there. Done. Story over. End game. I'm enlightened. *That's* a direct experience of value. *That* is the ErosValue of Reality.

It moves quarks to come together and create a proton or a neutron. It moves protons, neutrons, and electrons to create an atom. Atoms desire each other, and they create a molecule. There are unique configurations of desire and intimacy, which are unique elements. Macromolecules emerge from molecules, because there is a desire for molecules to make contact, to touch each other, to love each other, and to create a larger whole. And then, when you intensify the intimacy of macromolecules, they become cells.

Find it in yourself. When your desire intensifies, you are throbbing. Your heart's throbbing, your body's throbbing. You're quivering open. Your heart, body, mind—any one of the three or all of the three, take your wish—is quivering open, is throbbing open, is pulsing open. Your desire intensifies—your artistic desire, your creative desire, your embodied desire, your tumescence, your throbbing, your pulsing. You step inside and you've got value.

IN THE ECSTASIES OF DESIRE, THE SPLIT BETWEEN AUTONOMY AND COMMUNION DISAPPEARS

And in that value, I have this huge devotion to other. Other cannot be brutalized. Other cannot be tortured. Other cannot be excluded. Other cannot be indiscriminately ignored in any way. Because my desire is to make contact, and to experience intimacy, which is mutuality of pathos, and mutuality of purpose, and mutuality of recognition. We recognize each other, we feel each other, and we have the shared value: more Eros and more intimacy.

There is this implicit devotion in desire. Desire is both the healthiest form of narcissism: *I'm fully alive with myself,* it's the healthiest form of autonomy: *when I'm filled with desire, I am most in myself*—and it's the healthiest and most whole form of devotion: *I'm utterly devoted to you.*

In the ecstasies of desire, the split between autonomy and communion disappears. There is no ethnocentrism. There is just the Field of Eros. There is just the Field of Desire. That's the code of desire of Cosmos. That's what Cosmos is.

I am that desire. Not *tat tvam asi,* "thou art that," in the sense of I am *just awareness.* No, no, no. That's a mistake. It's why I've argued against that for the last twenty years. I am not *just* awareness. I am the Field of *ErosDesire.* And *ErosDesire* is the field of *ethos.* I know that because I am madly loving you. I know you. I recognize you. To recognize is to know. I know you. I see you.

LoveEros is a perception. That perception arouses my love, and my love then arouses my perception. Love and knowledge become a circular movement. Eros and gnosis. *Ya'da means* "to know" and "to love." *Ya'da:* to *know* value, *Ya'da:* to *see* value. To love is to see, to perceive value.

It's so deep. Reality is a code of desire. That's what Reality is. The Eros equation and the intimacy equation are codes of desire.

REALITY IS DESIRE: THE NAME OF GOD

What we're doing together is telling this new Story of Value. What is a new Story of Value? It is the best code of desire that we have available based on the best sciences in Reality today.

The great Islamic thinker Rumi understood this so well, and Hafiz understood this so well. But remember a text from the thirteenth century from the *Zohar,* which says, *Histakel be-'Oraita u-bara 'alma,* "She gazed (that's an erotic gaze) at the Torah (the sacred text), and she manifested Reality." And what is the sacred text?

In the lineage tradition of Solomon, *the sacred text is the names of God*, writes Nachmanides in the thirteenth century. *All of sacred text is nothing more and nothing less than a particular code of the names of God.*

Now what's the name of God? Let's take another look.

Hei   Vav   Hei   Yud

This is the name of God. The first letter in the name is *Yud. Yud, Hei—Yah*, as in Leonard Cohen, *Hallelujah. Hallel* is the ecstasy of *Yah—*of the *Yud* entering the *Hei*.

There is a dimension of the Divine that's beyond all names. But then, Infinity, the infinite no-thingness, discloses as the *Infinite Intimate*. Divinity is not only witness and aware of all. Divinity is the stirring of desire. One of the qualities of the Infinite is the desire for intimacy with the finite. So the *Yud* enters the *Hei—Yah*. Yah is the two letters *Yud* and *Hei*. This is called in the Book of Radiance *Zivug Matmedet*—constant erotic union.

Breathe in. Then, on the outbreath, *Yah!* That's the breath of Reality. Breathe in, then *Yah!* The *Yud* enters the *Hei—*and that is the constant Eros of Reality. That is Reality that is intimacy, that is the Intimate Universe. That's the field of electromagnetism. It's the strong and the weak nuclear forces. It's the gravitational forces, all of the Higgs-Boson fields. It's all the leptons, hadrons, and muons. It's the whole thing, pulsing in Reality in this very moment.

And then, the second two letters of the four-letter name of God is *Vav, Hei*. The *Yud* pulled down is a *Vav*, and the *Vav* enters the *Hei*. The line enters the circle, the *Vav* enters the *Hei*. That's the arousal of the Field of Desire. That's my participation in the code of desire. That is Conscious Evolution. When the code of desire of Reality becomes uniquely conscious in me and in my life, through my code of desire and my conscious ability to up-level, evolve, and deepen my own code of desire, I participate in rewriting the code of desire of Reality.

This is called by the Book of Radiance: *Zivug she'eino mat'medet*, erotic union which is not constant but aroused by human participation.

- ◆ The *Yud* enters the *Hei*—the electromagnetic field, all the four forces.
- ◆ The *Vav* enters the *Hei*—the Field of Eros, the Field of Desire, desire for intimacy, come consciously alive uniquely in the human field. Both personally in my life, in my codes of desire, and in the cultural codes of desire that define the *polis*, that define the politics of Reality.

Of course, we need politics of Eros. We need a culture of Eros—and a culture of Eros means a culture rooted in a shared code of desire.

THE FIELD OF DESIRE LIVES IN ME

We have this Aramaic text that says *histakel be-'oraita u-bara 'alma*: "She gazes at the Torah, and She manifests Reality." And what's the Torah? Names of God. Torah is the name of God. Wow! Just feel that with me for a second. Feel that with me.

But the Torah is one particular code of desire. It's one particular way of writing the name of God. There is no split between me and the text. I am the Torah, and I am the great literature of the Sufis, and I am the great literature of the best of the Jesuits and the Desert Fathers.

My *I* is a unique code of desire that participates in the code of desire of the whole.

Let's see the name of God again, but this time embodied in the human being:

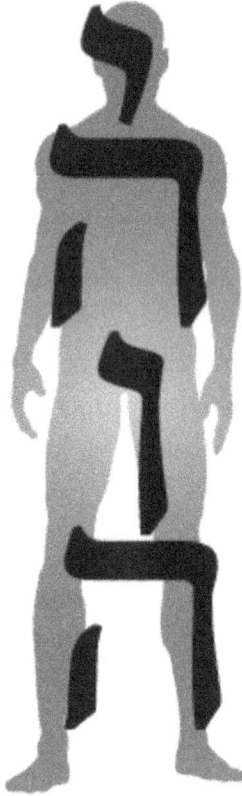

Man in the Image of IHVH

That's a human being, a person. For the lineage masters, the *Yud* is the head. The head enters the upper carriage, shoulders (the *Hei*). The *Yud* enters the *Hei*. The *Vav* is phallus or yoni—that dimension of the human being, which is phallus, yoni, line, circle that lives in every human being. It enters the *Hei*, the lower carriage of the human being.

The point of the image is that *I am the name of God,* which means *I participate in the Field of Desire.*

I am not separate from the Field of Desire. There is a Field of Eros, there is a Field of Desire, and I don't just live in the Field of Desire—the Field of Desire lives in me. I *am* the Field of Desire. My code of desire influences the entire field.

That's what we mean by Conscious Evolution. It means the Field of Desire becomes awake and alive in me.

My journey of transformation is a journey to rewrite my unique code of desire, which is my Unique Self. My Unique Self is my unique Torah. My unique Torah, my unique Rumi poem, my unique letter in the cosmic scroll of desire. My Unique Self is my unique code of desire. My unique code of desire is evolution becoming uniquely conscious through me. That's what *Conscious Evolution* means.

Let's step out of our heads. Just feel it in your body, because the code of desire cannot be disembodied. The body is insufficient, but the body is absolutely necessary.

The body is a quivering, pulsating Field of Desire. That's what the body is.

The early psychoanalysts pointed out what all of the great wisdom traditions knew, what the great Islamic mystics knew, and the great Hebrew mystics knew, and at their best, Magdalene mystics knew. The body is "polymorphously perverse."⁵ And "polymorphously perverse" means *the body is a Field of Desire.*

The baby desires to be held in the arms of the mother. The baby desires to touch and to be touched.

When we can live in the goodness of that Field of Desire, we have direct access to knowing, to truth.

---

10   Polymorphous perversity is Sigmund Freud's descriptive term for the non-specific nature of childhood sexuality in its primordial form.

EROSVALUE IS THE LOVEINTELLIGENCE AND LOVEBEAUTY AND LOVEDESIRE OF REALITY

Everyone's got their own unique configuration of desire. But I've got to be in the Field of Desire. When I am in the goodness of that desire, I realize there is no split between love and desire. **And there is no split between love and intelligence—because intelligence is not technical; intelligence is the omni-considerate movement of Reality towards ever deeper contact and ever greater wholeness.** That's intelligence. Intelligence is the depth, the unimaginable, stunning, erotic beauty of a proton, which is *not* three quarks, although three quarks become a proton. But a proton is an entirely *different* Field of Intelligence. It *is* a Field of *Eros*Intelligence.

It *is* a Field of ErosValue.

A proton is a new quality of Eros that can potentiate new Reality that is erotically potent in new ways, that can generate new possibilities of life. That's the intelligence of a proton. It is a LoveIntelligence, but that LoveIntelligence is bound up, intimately and intricately inter-included in a LoveDesire. The proton *desires* the neutron, and together, they desire the circling of the electron.

That's how an atom comes into being.

LoveDesire and LoveIntelligence are filled with mad beauty that includes all contradictions. **Because that's what beauty is: all opposites become woven together in a larger paradox of intimacy;** *shared identity* **in the context of** *otherness.* That's the ultimate paradox, which is the ultimate beauty—because **beauty is the holding of paradoxes.**

Read Whitehead's *Process and Reality:* it's an unreadable book, but read it anyways. **He understands correctly that beauty is all of the contradictions woven together into this stunning whole.** And I'm with him; I've always understood beauty that way. I was sharing this understanding of beauty, and someone referred me to Whitehead suggesting that he had come to a similar conclusion. Indeed he had. It's good to meet fellow travelers on the path.

The LoveIntelligence and the LoveBeauty and the LoveDesire of Reality—that's ErosValue. It lives in me, as me, and through me. That is the name of God.

MY UNIQUE NAME OF GOD EMERGES FROM MY UNIQUE CONFIGURATION OF DESIRE

Rabia, the great Islamic erotic mystic, says, "*One day He did not leave after kissing me.*" When Rabia says *He did not leave*, she means that her experience of *her* name was the name of God, the name of She. And yet that name is not generic; *the name of God that inheres in me, that I incarnate, is unique.* She writes that everyone has to find their own name of God.

I am a unique configuration of desire, and that means I am a unique name of God. I have a unique way to call God. Can you feel that?

Rabia writes, *Would you come if someone called you by the wrong name?* When we are about to explode, after we've crossed that line in sensuality, and we call our beloved's name and our beloved calls our name, would you come if someone called you by the wrong name? You can understand and feel the textured nature of that writing.

> *I wept because for years He did not enter my arms.*
> *Then one night I was told a secret:*
> *Perhaps the name you call God is not really His, not really Hers.*
> *Maybe it's just an alias.*
> *I thought about this and came up with a pet name.*
> *I came up with a pet name for my Beloved I never mentioned to others.*

All I can say is, it works!

Your pet name for God is the name for God that moves out of and emerges from your unique configuration of desire—as a unique name of God that never was, is, or will be ever again. This is your direct participation in the Field of Value, where you know value to be true, and value knows you.

That's your unique code of desire. **Your unique name of God**—the pet name that you call the Divine, your own nickname given to you by *She* that loves you so—*that's* **your unique code of desire**. Your unique code of desire is the unique name of *She*, of *He*, that lives in you, as you, and through you.

EVOLUTIONARY LOVE CODE: EROS AND GNOSIS ARE NOT SEPARATE

A wise man once said:

When we feel, we can begin to think.

And only then can we begin to engage in the sensuality of sensemaking.

Love and knowledge are not separate.

Eros and gnosis are not separate.

What we think is less than what we know.

What we know is less than what we love.

What we love is so much less than what there is.

And to that precise extent, we are in practice so much less than what we are in reality. [6]

To be what we are [truly], we need to love.

---

11 Referring to a quote from R.D. Laing.

We only know what we love.

We only love what we know.

When we know, we can begin to feel.

TO BE WHAT WE ARE, WE NEED TO LOVE MADLY

Our Evolutionary Love code says, "*What we think is less than what we know, and what we know is less than what we love.*" Loving is a deeper form of knowing.

"What we love is so much less than what there is, and to that precise extent, we *are* [in practice] so much less than what we are [in potential]." To be what we are, we need to love. **We need to love every moment open. And I can only love the moment open through my unique code of desire.**

In other words, my unique code of desire is my unique gift to this unique moment. And it's only me in this moment that can love this moment open within my circle of intimacy and influence, that no one else in the world can love open. I am living in my unique circle of Eros, my unique circle of desire, my unique circle of intimacy and influence. And my unique circle might be my immediate family. It might also be my place in the Unique Self Symphony, to participate in the evolution of love.

My unique code of desire is my unique capacity to love this moment open in a way that no one that ever was, is, or will be, can do.

My name is a unique name of God, and my name participates in the name of God. The name of God is *misspelled* if my name, my letter, is not in the name of God; it's distorted. I have a unique gift to give to *She.*

Raba Emunatecha, the text of the lineage, is usually translated, "Great is my trust in You, God." But the same words bear an equally accurate meaning: "Great is Your trust in *me*, God." *She*, the name of God, trusts me to live my name. So the words mean both *"Great is my trust in You, God"* and *"Great is Your trust in me, God."*

This is why when we make love, we call out the name of the beloved. And again, *making love* doesn't mean a formal act of a particular kind of coitus:

- Making love means I'm kissing your shoulder.
- Making love means we're looking in each other's eyes.
- Making love means you're kissing my belly.
- Making love means just kissing your hand in that one moment.
- Making love means we are deep in creating Reality together, heart-to-heart, in the palace of Holy Imagination.

To be what we are, we need to love—and love madly. Because we only *know* what we love madly. The only sanity is to love madly.

We only love what we know. And when we know, we begin to feel. Because the Universe is *LoveIntelligence*. The Universe feels, and the Universe feels love. It's only when I *know* that I can begin to *feel*.

When we begin to feel, we begin to think. A scientist can't disclose the intelligence of Reality unless they're madly in love with truth. There's a wild, ecstatic love in science. Wow! Steven Weinberg talks about how he cannot find the point of the universe, and then, in the next sentence, he talks about how he is madly in love with knowing the truth of muons. When he's looking for the point he can't find, he is *thinking* about the point—and he is rebelling, correctly, against old fundamentalist religions. What he didn't realize when he wrote that is that:

There is a deeper cosmic Story of Value, which is a Story of Desire. That Story of Value is his—Steven Weinberg's—**desire to know the truth of**

muons, and to uniquely contribute it to physics, in a way that no one else that ever was, is, or will be, could.

I have a unique gift to give, which is my unique code of desire. To the precise extent that I am alienated from my code of desire, I'm taking the name of God in vain. This is because:

1. God is value.
2. Desire discloses value.
3. Unique desire discloses unique value.
4. My unique code of desire discloses the unique name of God.
5. Therefore, to be alienated from my unique code of desire is to be alienated from my unique value, which means that I am not pronouncing the unique name of God that lives in me, as me, and through me, and this is what it means to take the name of God in vain.

I am a sacred text. A sacred text is a code of desire. But I have to be constantly *rewriting* my sacred text, constantly *evolving* my sacred text, constantly evolving *my name*. Only then we can begin together to engage in the sensuality of sensemaking.

EVEN AS WE ARE ALL UNIQUE, WE ARE ALL THE SAME

Love and knowledge are not separate. Eros and gnosis are not separate.

We have unique codes of desire, and yet we participate in the one desire. We are radically unique, and yet we are the same, which is why we can talk to each other. It's why we understand each other now. It's why we have the shared field together. It's why we are not ultimately lonely—because there is a one Eros in which we all participate.

Everything we've talked about today, we recognize it inside of ourselves. There is not one word I shared today that was new, that you, we, didn't recognize living in some way inside of us. Even though each one of us might have heard this *dharma* uniquely, we come together in intimate communion, because we also heard it together.

Because even as we are all unique, we are all the same—that's one of the First Principles and First Values of Reality—**which is why we can have** *common sense:* **because we have a common** *sensuality.*

Because there is actually one desire, and one Eros, and one value, and one breath, and one love.

CHAPTER EIGHT

COSMOEROTIC HUMANISM: TRANSITIONAL OBJECTS, EVOLVING CODES OF DESIRE, AND THE NEW HUMAN AND THE NEW HUMANITY

Episode 372 — November 26, 2023

TO HEAL REALITY, WE MUST HEAL OUR NARRATIVES OF DESIRE

To heal Reality, we have to heal our narratives of desire, our stories of desire—and we can't split desire from sexual desire. The desire of the sexual is the model for Eros. The sexual models the erotic. It doesn't exhaust the erotic, but it models Eros. When we have broken stories of desire in the sexual, then we have broken stories of desire in the political and in the economic. **When we have broken stories of desire, we have broken stories of value.**

Just like we need to heal the abuse of the sexual—the sexual abuses that have run rampant in the world, which are the abuses of desire, the distorted and degraded codes of desire in the personal— **we need to heal the abuse of the sensual and the abuse of desire, the degradation of our shared codes of desire in the political and in the economic.** We need to heal the body, and we need to heal the body politic.

We need to evolve the quality of Eros and desire as it lives *in me, as me, and through me. I need to go back and recover the native innocence of my desire*. Not a *first* innocence, but after I've gone through everything—all of the complexity, all of the guilt—I get to a *second* innocence. And I know that I am always already pure and beautiful. After I've gone through all the tragic, I get to the post-tragic, and I feel the beauty and the wonder of my inflamed desire.

Just as I do that in the personal, I need to do it in the political. **The early feminists weren't wrong when they said, "the personal is the political." We'll just add that "the political has to be *the cosmic*."**

We can only have a politics today that is a politics of Eros, rooted in a realization that there is a shared Field of Desire, and the shared Field of Desire is a shared Field of Value, and that we all can access it. Hope is a memory of our common sense, which is our common Field of Value.

Hope is a memory of value that lives ever already in us, as us, and through us, in our bodies themselves.

It's only when we're not listening to the murmurings of Eros—which are the murmurings of the sacred in the body, which is the story of value, the code of desire intrinsic to Cosmos—**that I have to write false codes of desire.**

Every form of degraded ideology is a false code of desire. Every sacred text that speaks against the intrinsic nature and Eros of cosmic value and cosmic desire is idolatry. **Idolatry is false codes of desire.**

Everything we are doing is about codes of desire. **The more I rewrite and evolve and clarify my own code of desire, the more I can participate as da Vinci.** We can be da Vinci together. The lead author of all of our work is David J. Temple, a pseudonym we created. **We can be David J.**

Temple together, and we can write the new library. We can write the Great Library of value because we *become* clarified value.

We *become* clarified desire.

HOW DO I CLARIFY MY OWN CODE OF DESIRE?

Next we're going to discuss: *How do I, in my own life, clarify my own code of desire—erotically, sexually, creatively?* The code of my body: my body's psyche, and my body's drama, and my body's history, and my body's trauma—because there is no love story without the transformation of trauma. The transformation of trauma is core to the love story. This is why in the lineage, we talk about the shattering of the vessels, the breaking of the vessels, which precedes the Eros of manifestation of the Universe: A Love Story.

We are going to talk about how we go into our own codes of desire as *Homo amor,* to participate together in writing the new codes of desire at this moment, at this time between worlds and time between stories.

At the core of the new Story of Value are codes of desire. We talked about codes of desire in Reality, and the relationship between Eros, desire, and existential risk. Now we're going to talk about our own codes of desire: **how healing my own code of desire**—which has to do with my sexual narrative—**transforms my life.**

We are going to talk about how the healing of my own personal code of desire also heals the meta-crisis and directly addresses existential risk. **Healing the code of desire in my body is what heals the body politic.** Healing the code of desire in my personal story is what heals culture. Healing my own stories of abuse heals the abuse in culture.

Making myself whole makes culture whole.

We are going to try and articulate the deepest understanding we can of the new Story of Reality.

HOMO ARMOR TO *HOMO AMOR*

What does it mean to become a new human? Because it's only when I become a new human that we can create the new humanity.

What's my personal code of desire?

How do I evolve it to become whole, to become the new human?

What's my personal code of desire, and how do I evolve it to move from being Homo armor—the armored human being who can't access their code of desire—to becoming Homo amor, to becoming powerful beyond measure?

Because my own unique desire is the source of my joy, and the source of my power, and the source of my ethics, and the source of my delight. We feel the agony and the ecstasy. We laugh out of one side of our mouths, and we cry out of the other side of our mouth.

I just read this morning an incredibly painful story about two doctors who were killed in Gaza, trying to take care of their patients in an impossible reality. Every day, I feel and see the faces of young boys—eighteen, nineteen, twenty year olds—who are in the impossible position of protecting Israel after October 7th, which was probably the largest public rape, sexual abuse, murder, snuff film violence, publicly played out in the history of the world.

And now Hamas is tragically holding the doctors hostage, the beautiful Palestinian doctors in Gaza, who died as absolute, gorgeous heroes. At the core of Hamas is a failure of a love story. It's a failure to access a code of desire that's aligned with the nature of Reality, with Goodness, Truth, and Beauty.

At the very core of the jihadi worldview is a degradation of desire, of the dignity of desire—the desire of the body, the desire of sexuality—and an incapacity to hear the murmurings of the sacred, the murmurings of desire, in the other, in the one who's outside of the jihadi worldview.

WHO I AM IS DESIRE, AND DESIRE IS THE PLOTLINE OF MY LIFE

Reality, at its core, is desire. That's what Reality is. That's how we begin. At its very core, Reality has appetites. In the words of Alfred North Whitehead it has *appetition*. The lineage of Solomon uses the word *teshukah*: a central desire that throbs at the very heart of Cosmos itself. I was privileged—in a couple of academic works called *Radical Kabbalah*—to unpack the lineage sources of the wisdom of Solomon. There is a section in the first volume, on this throbbing, pulsing, dripping, tumescent *teshukah*, the desire at the very heart of Reality. This is why Reality doesn't stop with hydrogen: "*Oh, we've got hydrogen, let's stop, in the first nanoseconds, in the first moments of time.*" But Reality desires more. Reality has an incessant desire for more life, and more value, and more wholeness.

What we're trying to do to heal culture—at this moment of meta-crisis, in this time between worlds and time between stories—is access and articulate the intrinsic desires of Reality.

The desires of Reality are the plotlines of Reality, because my desire is the plotline of my life. **I am desire.** That's who I am. Desire is not *extraneous* to who I am. It's not an accident. **It's my very essence. The emergent possibility of human consciousness that now needs to come online**—in order to heal culture and respond to the meta-crisis—**is to become aware that "Who I am is desire, and desire is the plotline of my life."**

MY DESIRE IS SACRED

What do I desire? I desire *value*. We always desire value. Desire is always desire for value; pseudo-desire wants pseudo-value. I desire a value that's not here, that's not available. "*I want that.*" That *want*—that *teshukah*, that *appetite*—is sacred, it is holy.

> *Eros is the experience of Reality desiring ever deeper contact and ever greater wholeness. That's the code of desire that's inherent in Reality itself.*

At different points in history, different social groups—different communities, different churches, different religions—tried to articulate codes of Reality to create what they felt was the best possible world, but those codes were almost never the *universal* codes that live in the structure of Cosmos itself. **Each religion intuited *some* value of Reality, and then built its system around that value.** Christianity built its system around forgiveness, and that became its value.

But there is a whole pantheon of values, which are all desired by Reality. Those are the First Principles and First Values of Reality. Reality has First Principles and First Values that are desired by Reality itself. Those are the codes of desire that live in Reality.

Local religion by itself won't take us home. Local culture won't take us home. We are challenged by existential risk, which requires global coordination, because every existential risk is global.

1. Global coordination requires global coherence.
2. Global coherence means we've got to resonate with each other, like musical instruments resonate with each other.
3. We need global resonance.
4. To have global resonance, we need intimacy with each other.

We need *global intimacy*—and we're now experiencing what we've called *a global intimacy disorder.*

How do we articulate global intimacy? In the same way we always create intimacy—in every couple, in every organization, or in every community. We can only create intimacy when we have a shared Story of Value. **It's only a shared Story of Value that generates intimacy. If we don't share a ground of value, then we can't have a shared vision.** We cannot go to the same place together. We cannot do sensemaking together. We cannot evaluate if we are not in a shared Field of Value. We can't do a shared evaluation of Reality if we are not in a shared Field of Value.

If we are not in a shared Field of Value, we can't have global intimacy, so we have a global intimacy disorder. We have no resonance with each other. We have no global coherence, and so the global challenges, which require global coordination, aren't met. Millions of people unnecessarily died in Covid, a relatively minor catastrophic risk, because of our incapacity to create global coordination, because we didn't have a shared Field of Value, and so we didn't have shared intimacy.

What we're doing is articulating the plotlines of a Reality story, which is Reality's codes of desire—the clarified codes of desire of Reality that we all share—that we all participate in.

At the global level, individual countries articulate false narratives— narratives of pseudo-desire, narratives of pseudo-eros, which are actually not erotic. They are dissociated or alienated from the whole: "*My country should dominate*"—whether "my country" is the Chinese Communist Party, or the original Mongol horde, or European colonial powers, or a particular tribe in Africa that brutalizes other parts of Africa. **We have win/lose metrics, in which every culture, every community, every nation, every**

religion is lost in its own ego self. It's dissociated from the whole. It tells a false narrative about itself, which places itself at the center. It becomes a hungry ghost for its own fulfillment, and is unable to feel the whole. The win/lose metrics generate broken fragile systems, which are the root cause for existential risk. We need to heal the broken codes of desire of culture.

THE BEGINNING OF HEALING BROKEN CODES OF DESIRE IS HONORING DESIRE

We need a way, shared by all of humanity, of healing our own broken codes of desire. We need a way to heal our own broken codes of desire, which means to create a new human. We need a way to heal the broken codes of desire of culture, which means to create a new humanity.

The beginning of that healing is the honoring of desire.

That's where it begins:

- ◆ I've got to honor desire.
- ◆ I've got to feel the goodness of desire.
- ◆ I've got to feel the dignity of desire.
- ◆ I've got to realize that Reality Itself is desire, and that desire is a force that needs to be deeply listened to.

Desire is the language of the Divine. Desire is the language which discloses value. All value is disclosed by desire.

We need the *clarification* of desire—knowing what I *truly* desire, both as a nation and as an individual—**so we can share a global "deepest heart's desire," which is made possible because we have a shared Field of Value.** Then we can heal the global intimacy disorder, which then heals culture.

We create a sense of being omni-considerate for the sake of the whole. We can *feel* the whole. We're not isolated. We're not lost in a cancerous narcissism.

We can actually feel each other's desire.

We can feel each other's hunger.

We can feel each other's pain.

We can feel the two doctors in Gaza.

We can feel the young Israeli boys. No one is split off.

Everyone's throbbing desire is for a shared Field of Value.

Every religion, every country can be a unique expression of the Field of Value, a unique instrument in the symphony of value and ErosDesire—but we are all part of the same music, and the music of Reality is ErosDesire itself.

What I want to turn to is a shared code that can be used by every nation, by all of humanity, by every human being.

TO BE IN JOY IS A DIRECT BYPRODUCT OF ACCESSING THE UNIQUE QUALITY OF MY DESIRE

How do I heal my own personal broken code of desire?

What does it mean to heal my own broken codes of desire?

How do I become the new human?

How do I de-armor? How do I take off all that is blocking my ability to feel the unique clarity of my desire running through me, which leads me to my value?

Value is the plotline of my life. To know the value that's mine to pursue is to know the plotline of my life. I only know the plotline of my life if I can access the unique contours, the texture of my own desire.

We want to heal the broken narratives of desire in order to heal culture itself.

Desire lives in me. I participate in the Field of Desire. To be alive is to access the unique quality of my desire. **To be in joy is a direct byproduct of accessing the unique quality of my desire**—not my pseudo-desire, not my surface desire—**my deepest heart's desire, the depth of my desire.**

Both my dignity and my divinity are dependent on my capacity to access my Unique Self. My Unique Self is not my separate self. It's not my broken skin-encapsulated ego. **My separate self is caught in false narratives of desire**—desires that aren't mine, desires that were foisted upon me by algorithmic structures speaking to our lowest common denominator, desires that were thrust on me by broken church narratives, desires that were thrust on me by reductionist materialistic narratives of win/lose metrics.

All of these—combined with an unimaginable host of toxins, chemicals, pharmacology, broken environments, broken ingestions into the body of foodstuff that shouldn't be in the body, either the distortion of the body or the malnourishment of the body—**alienate me from my own code of desire.**

All of those together create a cultural trauma, which dissociates me from my Unique Self. I can't find the voice of my Unique Self. To find my Unique Self, I have to first step out of my separate self, step out of my skin-encapsulated ego, and feel the wider field. That's the first step — I feel the wider field.

.

I AM PART OF THE THROBBING FIELD OF EROS, WHICH DESIRES EVER DEEPER SHARED IDENTITIES

Feeling that wider field was often called *True Self*, or the Field of Awareness. We were told, *move beyond your story*. And I'm guilty, I taught this for years in my mid to late thirties. It was wrong—or it was true, but very, very partial. But we are told, *move beyond your story and access the pure Field of Awareness that lives in you, the pure Field of Consciousness.* To know that *Tat tvam asi:* "Thou art that." You are pure consciousness. That's precisely half true. It is true, gorgeously true. As Max Planck, the quantum pioneer said, *consciousness is fundamental to everything.*

But consciousness doesn't live by itself. Consciousness has an interior. And the interior of consciousness is desire.

It is Eros. Eros Value. There is no consciousness without Eros. Eros Value. To move beyond my sense of being a skin-encapsulated ego, a broken separate self is to access this larger field. But this larger field is not just a Field of Awareness or Consciousness. It's a Field of Desire. It's a Field of Eros. It's pulsing Eros. Eros is this pulsing Eros that desires ever deeper contact and ever greater wholeness.

Eros desires ever deeper intimacies, which means deeper and deeper shared identities—not fusion, but *unions*—deeper unions, deeper mutualities of recognition, deeper mutualities of embrace, deeper mutualities of value, deeper mutualities of pathos—*we feel each other*, deeper mutualities of purpose—shared purpose and destiny.

Eros moves separate parts into larger unions, with these mutualities, these ever deeper, gorgeous, and stunning intimacies. That is the Field of Eros. **I step in, and I realize "*I am part of this larger pulsating, tumescent, throbbing Field of Eros.*"**

That's the Story of Value that I live in.

That's True Self.

That's the beginning of the Story of Value, the story we call CosmoErotic Humanism.

THE PLOTLINE OF MY LIFE IS MY UNIQUE CODE OF DESIRE

Then there is the second step: I realize I'm not just living *in* this pulsing field. This field is pulsing *in me*. But this field is not just pulsing in me, it's not just throbbing in me, it's not just tumescent and spreading itself open to receive the penetration of Reality. No, actually, it's *uniquely* tumescent in me, it drips in me *uniquely,* it pulses in me *uniquely*. It throbs in me uniquely. I am a *unique* configuration of desire. I am a *unique* quality of desire that generates a *unique* quality of intimacy in Reality, that's unlike any quality of desire that ever was, is, or will be.

My story is *not* that which I move beyond. I move beyond my pseudo-story, my surface egoic story, my story based on win/lose metrics, beyond my story based on demonizing you, making you an *other*, seeking false forms of domination over you, false forms of status, placing you outside the circle, to give myself the illusion of Eros, the illusion that I'm inside the circle. All of those are false narratives. They are false codes of desire.

I need to realize I have a unique story. That story is my sacred autobiography. My sacred autobiography is my unique code of desire. My unique code of desire is that which I desire.

What I desire becomes the unique value of my life, the unique gift of my life, the unique expression of the First Principles and First Values of Reality, awake and alive in me.

That's my Unique Self.

That's my unique configuration of desire.

That's my unique pulsing and throbbing.

That's my unique story.

That's my sacred autobiography.

My sacred autobiography is the most true, and authentic, and stunning narrative of my life. It is my unique story. It is my unique love story, which is chapter and verse in the Universe: A Love Story. My unique Eros and my unique desire is the unique chapter and verse in the Field of Desire.

Not only do I live in the Field of Desire, the Field of Desire lives in me. **As I clarify my unique code of desire, I begin to realize my unique value, my unique gift, my unique ethos.** And I realize:

- ◆ I am here as a unique expression of the aliveness of the whole.
- ◆ I'm filled with the desire to give my gift to the whole, to serve the whole, to be in devotion to the whole's aliveness.
- ◆ I become omni-considerate for the sake of the whole.

But it all begins with clarifying my unique codes of desire. When I am in the field, and I have direct access to the field, and the field lives uniquely in me, that's my Unique Self, that's my unique configuration of desire.

When I am blocked, when I can't access the field in which I participate, then I can't know the plotline of my life. Because the plotline of my life is my unique code of desire.

THE MOTHER IS THE UNIVERSE: A LOVE STORY IN PERSON

Transitional objects become false codes of desire. In 1951, Donald Winnicott, an American theorist, wrote about *transitional objects*. What are transitional objects? "I am a baby. I am held in the field of the mother." *The mother* is both the biological mother (there is an enormous need for the embrace of the biological mother), and the mother is also *Mother*, the field of *She*, the Field of Eros that knows my name and holds me. *I feel at home at the breast of the mother. I feel at home when my body is enmeshed with the body of the mother*—which is why early childhood matters so much. But it's not dependent *just* on a biological mother.

Even if my biological mother was imperfect—as all biological mothers are—there is a larger Field of She which holds me.

It's Mother Nature. It's Mother as the Field of Value. It's Mother as the Field of Eros. It's Mother as the *Welcome Home* sign in Cosmos. **Mother is the experience that *I'm welcome in Cosmos*, that *I'm needed*.**

The existentialists of the mid-twentieth century tried to express their experience that they were no longer welcome in Cosmos. Camus' book, *The Stranger,* begins with the lines: *Mother died today, or was it yesterday?* Meaning, *there's no mother that welcomes me, and the death of the mother doesn't matter. The mother has died, and it doesn't matter. Because there is no Field of Value, and there is no Field of Meaning, and the world is random and happenstance.*

That was the existentialist travesty and trauma. All of existentialism was a failed—glorious, but failed—attempt to create meaning where there was none.

The mother is *the Universe: a Love Story* in person. The mother is— for those moments between baby and child—*Homo amor.* It's why breastfeeding is so important. *I can feel the livingness of the Divine*—which is why the Divine is often called *El Shaddai; El Shaddai* is the God who is the breast, in the lineage of Solomon.

I am held at the breast of the mother.

My desire is honored.

My body is "polymorphously perverse"—in a language of early psychoanalysis, from one of its best moments. This means *"My body is alive, my body is a personal incarnation of the living Universe."*

WHEN I NO LONGER FEEL THE BODY, I CREATE FALSE CERTAINTIES WHICH OVERWHELM ME

When I have that experience of the living, somatic goodness of Reality, when I feel my body pulsating Reality, when I feel completely alive, and Reality is self-evidently good, then what happens? The mother leaves. And when the mother leaves, I get desperately afraid. So what do I do? Winnicott says, *I take on a transitional object.*

A transitional object is something that I invest with the experience of being welcome in the Universe, let's say, a teddy bear or a security blanket. What's a security blanket? A security blanket is this object that I'm completely attached to, I am completely connected to it, I am desiring that object. If I lose that object, my heart crashes. I scream with pain. All of my desire and all of my yearning is for that object—to hold that object and to have that object hold me. That's a transitional object.

It begins as a teddy bear, it begins as a security blanket, or a puppy, but then, as I get older, that security blanket doesn't disappear, it just changes faces. That security blanket might become some version of my athletic prowess, it might be what I feel to be my beauty. My beauty becomes my transitional object, or my doctorate becomes my transitional object, or my relationship becomes my transitional object, or my child becomes my transitional object. In other words, I hold on.

- ◆ I'm not actually present.
- ◆ I'm not here.
- ◆ I'm not actually desiring you.
- ◆ I'm not desiring knowledge.
- ◆ I'm not *desiring*.

Everything I desire becomes a desire for a transitional object that gives me the illusion of feeling welcome.

It can be ideology, any form of ideology. That ideology becomes my transitional object, whether it be my commitment to communism, whether it be my battle against sexism or classism—even though those might be legitimate battles, but my battle against it becomes my transitional object. *My ideology becomes my transitional object.*

In other words, **when we no longer feel the body**—the body's pulsating Reality that welcomes me into the world—**then we create false certainties**. We create false transitional objects. We create pseudo-codes of desire.

These transitional objects become my new code of desire:

- They overwhelm me.
- They define me.
- They become a pseudo-identity.
- They become a false narrative of my life.
- They become a false code of desire.

These are the codes of desire that animate my heart, my body, my soul. They replace my ability to have direct access to my own Unique Self, to my own True Self, to the code of desire which is the sacred autobiography, my unique letter in the cosmic scroll.

WHEN MY DESIRE IS SHAMED, I CAN'T ACCESS THE GOODNESS AND ALIVENESS OF REALITY, AND I REACH FOR A TRANSITIONAL OBJECT

How do I access that unique letter, my unique code of desire, my sacred autobiography? To know how to access that unique letter, I've got to find:

- When did that get ruptured?
- When did I alienate from that?
- When did I lose access to it?

Almost always, it happened at a moment where my very embodiment, my aliveness itself was *shamed*. I had an experience of my own desire,

I had an experience of my Eros, an experience of my aliveness, and that aliveness, in some fundamental way, was shamed. Often, that shame incepts in the rejection of the embodied desire of a very young child for the pleasure of the body.

1. I have this experience of my body and my mother's breast. Either I'm held by the mother, or I'm yearning to be held by the mother.

2. I find my own body. My body seems alive. My body seems to be a gate to the intrinsic goodness of Reality.

3. And as I reach for my body in one way or the other, I have an early fundamental experience—which virtually every human being has—of being shamed.

4. That shame creates trauma. And trauma is but a modern word for the original religious word, sin. Trauma and sin are the sense that I'm not welcome in the universe, that *I'm not okay*. *Sin* came to mean: *I disobeyed God*. But at its core, the original impulse was: *I am not welcome. I can't feel my goodness. I can't feel the goodness of my aliveness.* In my earliest expression in the world, my goodness and my aliveness are completely connected, so my aliveness is shamed: *I can't feel my aliveness. My goodness is degraded.*

5. And so I lose my capacity to trust my body, I lose my capacity to trust the living verse, the story of my goodness and aliveness that lives in my body. I lose access to my own natural, unique desire. That unique desire is directed, restricted, denied, rejected, degraded, and so I have this experience that I can no longer trust the pulsing, coursing, dripping, throbbing currency of Reality that lives in my body. It's not trustable. I cannot trust my desire.

But remember, desire is not extraneous. Reality *is* desire, and I participate directly in the Field of Desire. **Who I am, my very essence, is my unique configuration of desire.** My unique configuration of desire is the unique plug that plugs into the Field of Desire and allows me to access the goodness and aliveness of Reality. That goodness and that aliveness are fully identified with each other.

And so, what happens? I look for a transitional object, which begins as a security blanket, but that security blanket invisibly up-levels, and transposes, and shifts. A transitional object is a shapeshifter; it shifts and it shapes, every person here can give it a different name.

Sometimes: "My son's approval becomes my transitional object." How could that be? How can a mother be dependent on her son's approval to live the fullness of her desire?

But sometimes, it reverses.

We start with wanting the approval of culture, of the parent, but often, the son or the daughter become the parent. That's one example. There are many examples, and we all know them.

I NEED TO RE-ACCESS DESIRE AS IT LIVES IN MY BODY

I need to be able to re-access my own desire. I need to first be able to re-access desire as it lives in my body, because my body is the Field of the Divine. This is critical.

We have four sexual narratives in Reality:

1. Sex-negative: "Sex is dangerous and gets you in trouble, stay away from it." The classical church narrative, that's one code of desire.
2. Sex-neutral: Kinsey: "Sex is basically like having lunch." How many people think that's true?
3. Sex-positive: "Sex is positive and sweet, and it's a panacea, and it creates good affiliation between people. It's this nice biological force that we can use positively." Nice, but bland,

and it doesn't capture the throbbing gravitas of the sexual.

4. Sex-sacred: "Sex is sacred, because it creates babies, because it creates life." That's beautiful, but when was the last time most people in the world had sex in order to create life? Most sexing in the world is not to create life. And much of the sexing in the world that does create life actually contradicts life because overpopulation is a major existential risk; it crosses our planetary boundaries.

We don't have a code of desire in culture to meet our own experience of desire. And our personal experience of our code of desire was degraded or rejected. Those two come together and traumatize the body, so now *I don't have direct access to a basic experience of my own goodness.*

Does everyone feel that? *I don't have direct access to a basic experience of my own goodness, and the goodness of my own story.*

And so, the pornographic universe enfolds me. The pornographic universe might be algorithms of pornography that direct my code of desire and hijack it, or that might be the pornographic universe of culture, in which I'm motivated by every buffeting sensation—in my drive for status, in all of the disguised forms of my transitional objects—and I can't find my way back to the body.

We have to find our way back to the body, back to the dignity of desire that lives in the body.

RECLAIMING THE LOST CODE OF THE BODY SACRED: THE SONG OF SOLOMON IS HOLY OF HOLIES

All of the sacred texts are holy, but they are not *Holy of Holies,* they are not the Temple. Holy of Holies, in the lineage tradition of Solomon, is the place of the Temple.

The unpacking we're about to do is lost; it is not available, it was hidden. But it's so deep, and it's so true. We need to reclaim it, and then evolve it, and merge it with the evolutionary sciences and with systems theory and complexity theory. But for now, I just want to give you two texts.

Text one, from the Wisdom of Solomon lineage: *All of the books are holy—* all of the sacred texts are holy—*but the Song of Solomon is Holy of Holies.*[7] What's the Song of Solomon?

I'll read you one fragment:

The fig tree puts forth her green figs.

Arise, my love, my fair one, and come with me.

His left hand is under my head, his right hand embraces me.

Drink of the juice of my pomegranate.

How beautiful and pleasant and gorgeous and stunning you are, oh loved one, with all of your erotic delights.

Your stature, your throbbing is like a palm tree.

Your breasts are like its clusters. I will climb the palm tree and take hold of its fruit.

May your breasts be like clusters of the vine, and the scent of your breath like apples, your mouth and your kisses like the best wine.

I am for my beloved, and her desire is for me.

Can you feel that? The text of the Song of Solomon is called Holy of Holies, which is the inner sanctum of the Solomon Temple.

The text of the Song of Songs is a text of desire.

That text of desire is the very nature of Reality Herself. **The Song of Songs reads** *tocho ratzuf ahava,* **"Its insides are lined with love"—with Fuck, with Eros, with tumescence.** It's the nature of Reality itself.

It's the dignity of my desire.

---

12 Rabbi Akiva, third century.

THE TEXT OF ETHOS IS WRITTEN IN THE BODY SACRED

I want to read you from this book, *A Return to Eros*, which is about these new texts of desire:

The text of ethos is written in the body sacred.

That's the new code of desire. Not "Sex should be ethical." Of course sex should be ethical! But sex is ethos. Eros is ethos. In other words, the quivering tenderness and the fierceness of the sexual desire contains within it a complete Bill of Human Rights.

Sex is ethics means our Code of Ethos is enfleshed in our bodies.

Sex is ethics means that the ecstatic urgency of the sexual contains within it all the principles of virtue and integrity.

Sex implies human rights. The exquisite beauty of the moist feminine open to penetration, the rawness of desire, the yearning to touch and be touched, to ravish and be ravished, to hold and be held, are all radical screams of Cosmos of our intrinsic dignity, of the essential truth that we are welcome in the Cosmos.

The radical pleasure and beauty of throbbing phallus and dripping yoni are democratized pleasures available to every human being, written in the code of every body sacred. These erotic capacities are not limited to the wealthier or the aristocratic or the particularly intellectual. **Every human being is personally addressed by an intensity of pleasure that cries out in affirmation of our infinite worth and dignity.** The Bill of Rights is encrypted in the code of desire that is our unique body.

The democratization of dignity has its source in the democratization of the dignity of desire.

In another text, the lineage writes that if all the books of wisdom would not be given, the Song of Solomon would be sufficient as source for all governance, for all politics, for all economics, for all wisdom. The Bill of Rights is written in the body sacred. The belly holds within it all ethos. The taut nipple, received in the mouth of the beloved, holds in it the infinity of the Divine: The dance of Yin and Yang, of Shiva and Shakti, of lines and circles, enfleshed, encrypted in the body sacred.

We all long to be poets. But we forget that we are already poems. **I don't really long to be a poet—I long to know that I *am* a poem.** I am a sacred text. And I am a unique sacred text, because I have a unique story.

The unique sacred autobiography, the unique narrative of my life, comes from my capacity to trust the direct knowing of my own intrinsic worth, which comes from my own anthro-ontological knowing. *Anthro*: my human body. Knowing what's real is ontology. I have direct access to the very goodness of Reality. I have direct access to the full field of *ethos*. I have direct access to the full Field of Value.

> *The entire Field of Value is written in the giving and receiving that is the play of the sexual, the play of embodied desire.*

Sex is divine desire in the body, uniquely expressed.

WHEN I ACCESS MY UNIQUE CODE OF DESIRE, I TRANSCEND THE PORNOGRAPHIC UNIVERSE

I can only transcend the pornographic universe when I begin to heal the trauma of being unwelcome in the universe, and I begin to feel and listen to the depth of my own unique experience of desire, when I begin to locate myself as CosmoErotic Humanism in person, when my body is aflame. But *aflame* can mean the most tender and gentle. My body is aflame with a desire to kiss my partner's shoulder, and that's enough. Sex doesn't look like one thing. The Field of Desire doesn't have one code. It's my *unique* code of desire. When I access that unique code of desire, I transcend (I end the trance of) the pornographic universe.

And by *the pornographic universe*, I mean not simply Pornhub, the actual incarnations of algorithmically generated codes of desire, but the pornographic universe of culture, which is filled with the transitional objects that alienate me from the true desires of my life, from my true gifts, from my true joy. Because my joy is a direct byproduct of my true gift.

Only when I access the unique code of desire, I can begin to heal the broken narrative of the abuses. It can be the abuses of culture that shamed me, which is one form of abuse. It can be the abuse which comes from the degradation of my unique desire, and my unique sense of being able to trust my body. That's another form of abuse, and that's abuse of the sexual. Or it can be classical sexual abuse. And what is sexual abuse? It means that somebody else made me an object in their own degraded code of desire, which was based on the violation of my code of desire. I became an object in someone else's degraded story, and then I can't access my own story. When I become an object, when I can no longer feel the dignity of my unique desire, when my unique desire is violated in sexual abuse, then I can't find my voice.

WHEN WE SPLIT OFF THE OTHER, WE VIOLATE THE DESIRE OF CULTURE

And then we violate the desire of culture. The desire of culture is the desire for a shared Field of Value. The desire of culture is the desire for global intimacy. The desire of culture is to transcend (to end the trance of) the global intimacy disorder, and to begin to experience ourselves together in a Field of Value.

How absurd it is that we live in a world that is entirely global and yet we don't have a shared Field of Value that we can live in together, and love in together, that we can feel each other in together, where we can actually experience the depth and dignity of the desire of every human being on the planet, and ultimately, the desire and dignity of the planet itself.

When we split off the other, when the other becomes an infidel, when the other becomes one who is tortured and raped and murdered to fulfill my code of desire, then we live in a world which is about to fall apart at its very seams, and its very fabric is ripped apart.

A materialist world is also a violation of the code of desire. There is the degradation of the code of desire by Hamas, which creates the jihadi culture of death—whether that was in Iraq with ISIS, or in Syria with ISIS, all having nothing to do with Israel, or in Gaza, when Hamas dominates the beauty of what should be a thriving Palestinian people. And there is a Western degradation of codes of sacred desire, which is *Barbie*, where there is no love story, no intrinsic code of desire. In that world desire itself is a social construction. There is no Ken and Barbie. It's all a tale told by an idiot, full of sound and fury signifying nothing. And Mrs. Mattel says to Barbie, *Humans just make up value, and then they die.* No!

Desire is the language of the Divine, and desire is enfleshed as you and as me. Through the enfleshment, desire embodies in you and me. *Through my body, I vision God*, writes the lineage. *Mi'besari echezeh Eloha.* My body is the code of desire.

THIS FIELD OF DESIRE IS THE PLACE WHERE I KNOW THAT I AM WELCOME IN THE UNIVERSE

And what do I desire? I desire value. And what value do I desire? I desire to come close to you. I desire to make contact with you. **I desire to gift you, the lover who is in the full thrust of intense desire.** She doesn't want to rape her beloved, she wants to ravish her beloved open to God, or open himself or open herself to be ravished open to God. Not *"fuck you"* as degradation, but *Fuck you* as in, *Let's Fuck each other open to God.* Let's love each other open to God, let's ravish each other into rapture. That's the desire that lives in the body sacred. This Field of Desire is the place in which *I know with absolute certainty that I am welcome in the universe. I can feel the welcome sign, literally coded in my body.*

My body is unique, and my desire is unique. And my unique desire is my message. But we are messengers who forgot our message. And what is my message? We are all messengers of the Divine.

> *I am a messenger of the Divine through the unique code of my desire, where I let my transitional object go, I de-armor, and I begin to be able to hear the unique voice of Homo amor, the new human.*

It is only through healing our story of desire, through enacting a new narrative of desire—*Sex Erotic*—that we can heal the body politic. And what is Sex Erotic? Sex Erotic is the knowing that the sexing that moves in me, that the desire that moves in me, is the desire of Reality, that the urgency that moves in me is not some pathology, or some violation of my good citizen self, or of my chaste religious self. No, my religion is my *religare;* my *religare* is my *connecting,* my re-ligamenting, my enfleshment with all of Reality itself, in which my body participates in the body politic. We need to democratize knowing. Every human being has direct access to the knowing that Reality is good, and that they are welcome in the universe.

To *know* you, to be a great lover, is to witness and feel your desire. *I am a great lover because with my eyes closed, I can feel where your desire is moving, and I can ride the Field of Desire with you, together.*

Because I feel you, and you feel me.

And I feel you feeling me, and you feel me feeling you. And I feel me feeling you feeling me, and you feel me feeling you feeling me. We begin to get these rivulets, these cycles, these spirals of ever intensifying and deepening desire.

And when we come to the ecstatic explosion of desire, we scream out, *Oh God*! We scream out the name of God, because we are in the Holy of Holies.

165

DESIRE IN ITS DIGNITY ALLOWED THE LINEAGE OF SOLOMON TO SURVIVE THE EXILE

I was in Dharamshala, and I had a deep dive meeting with my dear friend the Dalai Lama. We sadly don't talk often these years, because of the nature of where life is, and its intensities. But I was with the Dalai Lama, and we were in his back room, and he asked me how the lineage of Solomon survived the trauma and the degradation of the exile.

When the Temples of Tibet were destroyed, the Dalai Lama was—and remains—beside himself. *How do you perpetuate, when the Temple is destroyed, the ethos and Eros of your culture*, he asked me, *how did the lineage of Solomon do it?* And I cited to him the texts that we just studied together. *All the texts are holy, but the Holy of Holies is the Song of Solomon.* The Holy of Holies is no longer the physical Temple in Jerusalem, but it becomes the bed of desire.

> *The bed of the lovers is the new Holy of Holies.*

The people practicing the lineage of Solomon, even though they were degraded, and abused, and reviled, and trampled on, and therefore should not exist, yet they kept coming back to the marriage bed. They kept coming back to the dignity of desire. They kept coming back to the utter goodness of texts of desire written in the body sacred.

They did it imperfectly, and they did it in all sorts of ways that were complicated. But at the core, living desire kept them alive: desire for each other, desire for the sacred, desire for the sacred in each other, desire for the sacred everywhere.

At the core it was desire in its dignity that allowed the lineage of Solomon to survive the exile.

THIS NARRATIVE OF DESIRE MUST ARTICULATE A NEW STORY OF VALUE

And now, that narrative of desire—that lives deeply in the Song of Solomon and in the intuitive knowing of the Yab Yum in the Indian traditions, the dance of Shiva and Shakti, the yearning of yin for yang, the allurement that complexity theory understands to be at the heart of Reality, that desire which brings protons and neutrons and electrons to come together—**all of this has to form and articulate a new Story of Desire in its dignity.**

And what's the core dignity of desire? Desire desires value. *My deepest heart's desire is, I want to feel your desire.* The greatest gift you can give me is to let me see you in the quivering of your naked desire. I am not talking now here specifically about sexing; I am talking about Eros: *Let me see your open heart. Let you see my open heart.* To be a beloved is to witness the quivering desire of my beloved.

We—all of us, every one of us in the world—have to understand that in order to create a new body politic. We have to honor the quivering desire of every member and every tribe in the body politic. We have to feel into the desire of every human being. And how do you torture a human being that you just witnessed in the convulsing explosion of their entering heaven on the chariot of desire's dignity?

We have to heal. We have to heal and create a new Story of Value. And that new Story of Value is Sex Erotic. **Sex Erotic says that the sexual models Eros, and Eros is the Field of Ethics.** We have to reclaim the body in its goodness, and let the body mediate through the prism of the value which it desires.

That's what the lover desires. The lover always desires ever deeper contact. *When I am filled with desire for you, I am filled with devotion for you. I want to serve your pleasure. I want to serve your wholeness.* Every touch, every gesture, is alive and replete with meaning and infinity. **And I always scream your name, and then the name of God, and then *Yes!***

In every culture, we always say three things in the explosion of desire. We say *Yes*, we say the name of the beloved, and we say the name of God. Because **the *Yes* is the body sacred telling me that I am welcome in Cosmos**—and that every human being is welcome—**and that we have a shared Story of Value. And the name of the beloved and the name of God—I realize they're the same name; there is no split between them.** To be filled with desire is to see my beloved with the eyes of She.

This is the new story. This is beyond the transitional object. This is the new narrative of desire. We can't bypass the story of desire. We can't demonize codes of desire.

1. We need to recognize that every human being is a Unique Self, and a Unique Self is a unique code of desire.
2. We need to be in devotion and service to the emergence of the unique story, which is the unique value, which is the unique code of desire of every human being.
3. And from there, we create a Unique Self Symphony, where our codes of desire come together in a common story of value, omni-considerate for the sake of the whole. We understand that what unites us is so much greater than what divides us. We are fierce, and tender, and quivering desire.

My deepest heart's desire is: I want to make love with every human being on the planet. Not actually physically—that would take a while.

I want to have that experience of the Divine, and the divine field is personally addressing and making love with every human being.

That divine field lives in me. I'm an erotic mystic.

I want to make love with every human being on the planet. Not to enact that in physical sexing, but to be in mad devotion to every human being on the planet. I can feel their pain, and I can hear their desire, and I can taste their quivering. I honor—full honor, mad devotion—the divinity and dignity of their unique code of desire, and the unique code of desire of their people, and their unique instrument in the Unique Self Symphony.

That's the beginning of a new world.

That's the beginning of the healing of culture.

When we bypass desire, we create abuse: sexual abuse, political abuse, and racial abuse. We create all sorts of ideologies, and all sorts of *others* that we place outside the circle, to give ourselves the illusion of being alive.

Aliveness lives in us directly. It's available immediately. It's the democratization of greatness, which is the democratization of desire, and the democratization of the *dignity* of desire. That's the beginning: accessing my Unique Self is accessing my own unique code of desire, and knowing that my desire is desired by All-That-Is.

CHAPTER NINE

CLARIFIED FIRST VALUES AND FIRST PRINCIPLES GENERATE RIGHTS AND RESPONSIBILITIES

Episode 389 — March 24, 2024

EVOLUTIONARY LOVE CODE: CLARIFIED FIRST PRINCIPLES AND FIRST VALUES GENERATE RIGHTS AND RESPONSIBILITIES

Desire is the nature of Reality all the way down and all the way up the evolutionary chain. Clarified desire generates value. Clarified desire equals clarified need. As such, a clarified need is the need for value.

Or, said somewhat differently, evolution is love in action in response to need, or evolution is love in action in response to desire, or evolution is love in action in response to value. All three are different faces of the same Reality. Clarified value generates rights.

All First Values and First Principles—the plotlines of Cosmos—in their clarified form generate rights. Wherever there are rights, there are responsibilities. It is never only rights or responsibilities, but always rights and responsibilities.

Clarified First Values and First Principles generate rights and responsibilities.

Clarified First Values and First Principles are the new superstructure, which generates the new law, the new social structure. Law, which in postmodernity became dissociated from the Field of Value, now once again reclaims its pristine essence—as an expression of the Field of Value.

When I clarify my desire, I disclose value. Why? Because *my desire is not local*; there is no such thing as local desire. **All individuated, clarified desire participates in the larger Field of Desire.** There is no "local desire," no desires that are *only mine*—it doesn't mean my desires are *generic*; My desire is *unique* and *not local*; *I have a non-local unique desire*—*"non-local"* means that *my desire participates in the Field of Desire.* And that Field of Desire is one field, and it's one breath, and it's one love, and it's one heart, and it's one consciousness, and it's one desire.

But it is a *unique* desire. So, who am I? I am an irreducibly unique desire of the Field of Desire. It's not *just* my arousal, it's not *just* my throbbing, it's not *just* my tumescence. But it *is* actually my tumescence, my softness, the spreading of my heart and embodiment, the opening and the throbbing of my desire to love Reality open, thrusting deep into Cosmos and penetrating it with the depth of my consciousness and the depths of my being. *I am a unique expression of the larger field.* That is my unique desire.

If you have this desire burning in you—and it's a clarified desire, it's not a superficial desire, it's not your trauma acting out, it's what Barbara and I called *my deepest heart's desire*, what's called in the lineage *berur*—**this clarified desire participates in the Field of Desire.**

I access, in my interior, the Field of Desire:

1. I don't just live in the Universe; the Universe lives in me; I don't just live in a Field of Value, the Field of Value actually lives in me.
2. *Therefore, I can access the Field of Value. I can access the*

clarified Field of Value that actually lives in me.

3.   *The clarified Field of Value that lives in me expresses itself as my desire.*

4.   *I desire value. My deepest heart's desire is value.*

Now, value might mean life. Life is a value. Value might mean goodness. Value might mean Eros; Eros equals the experience of radical aliveness, moving towards, seeking, desiring ever deeper contact, and ever greater wholeness all the way down and all the way up the evolutionary chain.

The movement of Reality, of Eros, is towards deeper contact and greater wholeness, which is the value of Cosmos. This is why we don't talk about *Eros*, we talk about *ErosValue*.

My desire is for Eros, for ErosValue.

My desire is for intimacy.

My desire is for ever greater uniqueness.

My desire is for ever greater beauty.

My desire is for ever greater depth.

My desire is for ever more refined uniqueness, for ever deeper communion.

Clarified desire discloses value.

CLARIFIED DESIRE IS PRECISELY THE SAME AS NEED

We are now at the edge of the edge, literally, of culture itself. That's where we are. We are a little bit at the edge of the edge. It doesn't happen in Oxford and Harvard. It happens here. We're at the edge of the edge. Let's pour into each other. Let's be in full devotion, in the best purity we can muster. We're accessing Lionel Trilling's *Sincerity*. Let's be sincere, pure, and devoted as much as we can be together. What an unimaginable, mad delight and privilege to be in this conversation with you. Let's go to the next step.

Clarified desire is actually precisely the same as need. Desire and need are actually identical.

At the foundational levels of evolution, 380,000 years after the Big Bang, the desire of a proton and a neutron to come together to form a new whole, to have deeper contact and form a new whole of an atom: that is both a need, a primal need of the proton and the neutron, and it's a desire. I am using those terms not mythopoetically. I stake my life on that. This is not mythopoetic. That's the best description we can have of the interior face of Cosmos in which we participate, which participates in us. **That quality of need lives in me. That quality of desire lives in me.** There is an evolution of desire, there is an evolution of need, but need and desire animate Reality all the way down and all the way up the evolutionary chain.

THE NAME OF GOD IS DESIRE REACHING FOR THE FUTURE

The name of God in the lineage of Solomon realization is *Yud, Hei, Vav, Hei.*

Hei   Vav   Hei   Yud

Yud and *Hei* together make the sound *Yah*, as in Leonard Cohen's "Hallelujah"—it's the breath of Reality. It's the *Yud* entering the *Hei*—the yang and the yin, the upper waters and the lower waters, the Shiva and Shakti, the masculine and feminine, the line and circle that come together in Eros—that's the first two letters of the Divine name. The second two letters are the *Vav* and the *Hei*. The *Vav* entering the *Hei* is also an expression of erotic union. **The name of God is the experience of desire; YHVH. It's the experience of desire itself reaching for the future.**

The *Yud* enters the *Hei*—*Yah*. The *Vav* enters the *Hei*—*Va*.

Yud, Hei, Vav, Hei. Four letters. **But the first letter is a *Yud*, and *Yud* is the future.** That's what the name means.

It is pure Eros, the Eros of Cosmos, the allurement of the CosmoErotic Universe: protons, neutrons, electrons, the whole biosphere, and then into the human world.

- *Yud, Hei* is essentially allurement in the world of matter.
- *Vav, Hei* is allurement in the world of upper mammals and into the human world.
- *Yud* is the future.

That means: **the name of God is the *ErosValue* of Reality**—pure Eros, pure erotic union, the *ErosValue* of Reality—**reaching for the future.** That's what the name of God is, literally, and that name of God was probably the most influential category forming the western Renaissance, and with an enormous impact in the East as well. *Yud, Hei, Vav, Hei,* this four letter name of God, is the interior science monadic structure of Reality, which is desire for future value. That's the name of God.

All of Reality is names of God. All of Reality is in the Field of Value. All of Reality desires future value.

That's the core of the lineage of Solomon. But it also happens to be the core of Whitehead, who talks, in *Process and Reality*, about Reality having an appetite for value, for Goodness, Truth, and Beauty—Beauty being the highest value of all, which includes Goodness and Truth.

To be clear by the way, I'm not a Whitehead reader. I've taught and tried to unpack these ideas for many years, the last fifteen particularly, and then, four or five times, Whiteheadians would come to me and say, "Take a look at this, take a look at that in Whitehead." That's how I got to Whitehead. Then I corresponded with David Ray Griffin before he died. He was the leading Whitehead scholar in the world. He was a beautiful, beautiful man. I shared CosmoErotic Humanism with David. He said, "Whitehead essentially came to the same conclusion you did through a different door," which made me happy.

The name of God is desire reaching for future value. Clarified desire reaches for the future, meaning it reaches for a value, for something *I don't have now. I want something, I have a desire. It's my deepest heart's desire. It's not available in the present.*

CLARIFIED DESIRE AND NEED ARE COMPLETELY ISOMORPHIC

Now, at the foundational levels of evolution, desire and need are the same. Then we go up the evolutionary chain. We go into the world of biology, then into the human world.

And then, in the human world, there is a certain point where the human experience of being a separate self arises. It's a false experience: *"I'm just a separate self."* And I start experiencing my needs as my primal need to simply survive and my desires are something else. There is this moment where we think that needs are primal survival, and desires are extra stuff—creativity or whatever it might be. But that turns out not to be true. That's only an unclarified level of consciousness. **When I clarify my consciousness, I realize that, at the highest levels of evolution, just like at its foundational levels, need and desire are complete isomorphic.** They are identical.

175

One of the examples people give to split between need and desire at the middle levels of evolution is hunger strikes. A hunger strike means, *I give up eating for the sake of a higher value*, let's say freedom. They'll say, *Oh, I'm giving up needs for desires*, when that's actually not exactly true. No, **I am *clarifying* what my actual needs are.** I am clarifying that my needs are not only physical and my needs are not only survival. My *clarified* need is: *I need freedom.* Wow! There is a clarified need. And my clarified need and my clarified desire are isomorphic. They're identical. **Both at the foundational levels of the evolutionary chain and at the highest levels, need and desire are actually isomorphic.**

MY CLARIFIED NEED IS ALWAYS FOR VALUE

Now we can make a next step. My clarified need is always for value. **My need for food is for the value of life**—and there might be other values, there might be a value of Eros or pleasure, but the core value is life—**and I desire value**.

My clarified need and my clarified desire are the same.

Let's say I'm an artist. Is that a need? Or is that a desire? Well, it depends. There is a level at which it's not a need the way food is, but I might know myself so deeply that I need—like breath—this level of expression and depth. And without that level of depth, I actually die.

The movie *Cast Away* is about Tom Hanks who survives a cargo crash of FedEx. Tom Hanks figures out, on this beautiful island, a Caribbean-like paradise, how to master the neo-Darwinian thing; he's got all of his survival needs met. But he decides that he needs conversation, in which his interior meets the interior of another being. He tries using his blood to paint a face on a Wilson basketball, to see if that works. It didn't take him home, but it worked for a while. And then he decides he's got no choice. He needs to build a raft—he doesn't really know how to—and throw himself in the ocean on the one-percent chance that he's going to survive in order to fulfill this clarified desire—which is a clarified need—for one interior talking to another interior. Wow! It's a big deal. **The value of intimate communion—** which Tom Hanks feels on the *Cast Away* island—**it's not a *desire*. It's a *fundamental need*. It's a clarified need.** Clarified need and clarified desire meet as one, and it's always a clarified desire and a clarified need for value. That clarified desire, that clarified need, generates value. I am going to use the language of needs now.

Absolute need creates absolute ethics. *I need to breathe* becomes absolute ethics: *I have a full right to breathe.*

Now I want to make the leap. This is so important in law.

WE NEED TO GROUND RIGHTS IN FIRST PRINCIPLES AND FIRST VALUES

Law is supposed to be the place where value instantiates, but what's happened is **law has become dissociated from value**, which is why law cannot address, for example, TechnoFeudalism. Law cannot address Facebook, or TikTok, or Twitter. Law cannot address the entire technological world because law is based on precedent. The precedent is usually from an older world in which value was taken to be real. That value has been deconstructed, so precedent doesn't necessarily stand. Plus, technology is moving so fast that there is often no precedent.

Since law is dissociated from value, it's almost impossible to formulate relevant laws. Let me give you one example.

We've been talking about *attention hijacking* being at the core of TechnoFeudalism: the intentional deployment of machine intelligence to shape your desires and hijack your attention. There is, at this point, such an enormous level of very, very good literature on the damage that causes: depression, anxiety, destruction, polarization, the inability to place my sustained attention. We can't even read, let alone place our attention on issues that demand an educated democracy to formulate our future. And we certainly can't pay attention to the meta-crisis. We certainly can't pay attention to the future, place our attention on the future. This notion that attention is being hijacked—what's the weakness in that conversation? Why are all the books that criticize what we call TechnoFeudalism, the tech plex, why do they all fall flat? Why do they not move the tech plex? Because there is no formulated *right to attention*. **You have to *formulate* a right to attention.** There is currently no notion that *I have a right to attention.* So let's do that right now. I want to formulate, with you, a right to attention, a right to intimacy, a right to desire. Let me see if we can get it clearly.

Clarified desire equals clarified need.
Together they generate clarified value.
And clarified value is a right.

Eros is a First Principle and First Value of Reality, and one of the faces of Eros is desire. Desire is a First Principle and First Value of Reality. Reality *is* desire, or, as Whitehead said, Reality is appetite. **Reality is desire for value, so desire for value is a First Principle and First Value of Reality**, which is the response to a fundamental need—because clarified need and clarified desire are the same.

Evolution, at its core, is love in action in response to *need*. Evolution is love in action in response to *value*. Evolution is love in action in response to *desire*. All three of those sentences are different facets of the same diamond, different facets of the same ontological evolutionary truth. It's a big deal.

We realize:

1. Desire for value is a First Principle and First Value of Reality.
2. We've just completed a book formulating attention as a First Principle and First Value: the placing of attention is not a human creation; the placing of attention is a First Principle and First Value of Reality, all the way down and all the way up the evolutionary chain.

178

3. Intimacy is a First Principle and First Value of Reality.

There is a *right* to intimacy, and there is a *right* to attention, and there is a *right* to desire.

BILATERAL RIGHTS TO DESIRE—AND THEIR RESPONSIBILITIES

There are always rights and responsibilities. Rights never exist without responsibilities. You can't split rights and responsibilities. If there is a right to attention, there is a responsibility for attention. If there is a right to freedom, there is a responsibility in freedom. If there is a right to desire, there is a responsibility in desire. Rights and responsibilities always operate together.

Let's take a look at what a right to desire would actually look like. We are at the edge of the edge of the edge of the edge of the edge here. We are literally creating a new culture. We are creating new structures.

Let's say there is a right to desire. That means there is a right and responsibility, and it's bilateral:

I have a right to desire and I have a right to be desired.

That's a shocking thing to say. Obviously, we are not talking only about sexual desire. We're talking about the right to be desired as a human being, in all of my facets of my humanness. And I have a right to *desire* across all facets: to desire creativity, and to desire depth, and to desire Beauty, and to desire Goodness, and to desire Truth, and to desire embodied contact. These are fundamental rights and responsibilities. What that means is when I express my right to desire, I have to be responsible. I have to express my right to desire in a context that has mutuality, that has depth, that has respect, that has *ethos*, that has appropriate boundary, that has appropriate sensitivity. That's all true.

I have a right to desire, and I have a responsibility for how I express my desire. I have a right to be desired and a responsibility in how I articulate my being desirable in the world, how I action my being desirable in the world.

It's an interesting question.

For example, it's taken as an absolute given that it is patriarchal nonsense to suggest that a woman should walk with any level of modesty. Let's say, "breasts should not be almost fully exposed." If you say that, you are considered evil.

Now let's go really slow with this. Of course, there have been horrific statements like, "Oh, she was dressed like that, she had it coming." That's disgusting, horrific, not true, and evil. That's of course not the case. The way a woman or man dresses doesn't give anyone a right to behave to them in any particular way, certainly not a way that violates their boundaries and their mutuality. That's a given.

Having said that, if I know that a certain kind of dress generates a field of arousal—meaning, it generates a response to me in which I am desired—**I not only have a right to be desired, but I have a responsibility to how I express and articulate that experience of me being desirable.**

I am talking particularly now in the realm of the embodied sensual, but it would apply across *all* fields and ranges of desire. How I express my desirability is how I *seduce*—but not just seduce sexually, how I seduce emotionally, and aesthetically, and intellectually, and artistically, and economically, and politically. All of that requires rights and responsibilities. It's a big deal.

There are always rights and responsibilities.

They always live together.

I want to just stay with this for a second, just so we can kind of feel the full range of it.

One of the things our society has done is sought to coerce a particular kind of man and a particular kind of woman as this vision as *desirable* man and woman. And the other visions, they are fine, but they're not desirable. Is that a responsible expression of the right to be desired? Probably not. **We probably want to create a field of education and a Field of Value in which *every* human being experiences the utter and radical delight of desiring and being desired.**

We have a social, ethical responsibility not to impose cultural aesthetics, but to allow for free and open culture. Not to impose a cultural aesthetic which is homogenized, exclusive, elitist, and only available to one percent of the population, then the entire rest of the population lives yearning, *Oh, if I could look like that man or woman and be desired like that*. It's a big deal. But now let's go back to our major track.

FORMULATING RIGHTS AND GROUNDING THEM IN A FIELD OF VALUE

If there is a right and a responsibility, then we need to organize society in accordance with that right and responsibility. **For example, if there is a right to attention, then I don't have a right to steal your attention. It's a big deal. If there is a right to intimacy, then I don't have a right to violate your intimacy.**

You might think this is irrelevant, but it is actually the hottest issue in law: How do we formulate a right to privacy? There is an entire discussion now in the law reviews across the country about what the right to privacy means or doesn't mean, with an enormous amount of cases.

For example, there is one case that's gone to the Supreme Court, where the issue is: Does Google have a right to buy, from the University of Chicago Hospital, 212,000 medical records with detailed medical notes? Does the hospital have a right to sell those records without the approval of the patient? They are trying to figure out, *Well, why wouldn't they have a right to sell them?*

There is this appeal to the right to privacy. But then, in about seven or eight different legal articles I've been looking at the last couple of weeks, there is this discussion about what privacy is, and ultimately **privacy breaks down because virtually all of these articles are written by postmodern legal theorists, who basically say there is no intrinsic right to privacy.** It's got to be grounded in a larger right. This is what I have called in Mystery School teachings the right to desire and the right to intimacy.

One of my closest friends, students, colleagues, Venu, just completed a law review article called "The Right to Intimacy." He cites our book—*First Principles and First Values*—extensively to formulate a right to intimacy grounded in a Field of Value.

I've been talking about this in different ways for about seven, eight years. Venu is codifying it into these law review articles. He has done a very deep dive into dozens and dozens of legal articles in order to formulate this clearly. We're going to put out this article fairly soon.

This is just one example of the kind of move we have to make for the superstructure, the new Story of Value, to begin to reshape our story.

Whenever there is a core need, there is a core right. Need is the way Cosmos speaks. It's the way Goddess whispers. Goddess whispers in our ear through desire and need, which creates rights and responsibilities.

All of a sudden, we just brought together what we've called in earlier conversations superstructure and social structure. Superstructure is the new Story of Value. Social structure is, in part, the field of law.

We need to bring the new Story of Value—superstructure—and have it infuse social structure—law—in order to create a new kind of culture that can address technology and politics. That's what we're trying to do.

To sum up:

- Clarified desire generates value.
- Clarified desire equals clarified need.
- Clarified desire + clarified need (which are ultimately two faces of the same) generate clarified value.
- Clarified value generates rights and responsibilities.

This means that **the new superstructure of First Principles and First Values are the ground of a new social structure, a new system of law.**

DESIRE AND NEED ACTIVATE THE EYE OF VALUE

If we want to protect attention from being hijacked, it's not enough to write ten books screaming at the tech plex. I've got to establish firstly, there is an Eye of Value and secondly, there are First Principles and First Values. I've got to respond to postmodernity's legitimate critiques of value theory—which were important and good. I've got to resolve those critiques and then articulate a new notion of *evolving* First Principles and First Values.

First Principles and First Values are not fixed; they've got a basic ground, but then they evolve. There is an *eternal Tao* that's an *evolving Tao*. There are eternal values that are evolving values.

Within the Field of Value, I can access value. How? With the Eye of Value. How do I find the Eye of Value? What activates the Eye of Value? **What's the methodology of the Eye of Value? Desire and need.**

Desire and need disclose value.

It cuts beneath the Eye of the Mind; it's more primal. My deepest clarified need and my deepest clarified desire disclose value. And desire and need activate the Eye of Value.

I know everyone's like, "Oh, that's not realistic. It's not going to happen." No, no, the only thing that's realistic is that it will happen. Change is the only realism. The notion that it doesn't change is unrealistic. It always changes. We need to create the vessels, the structures, the horses that can actually carry the change. This move of superstructure downloading into social structure, an evolution of the source code, the new Story of Value reshaping the story of culture, is critical.

Of course, the example of attention is the most dramatic example. There are ten books that have been written in the last five-ten years, decrying stolen attention, but without being able to ground the objection in a Field of Value. Unless you can ground your objection to hijacked attention in the Field of Value—and you can actually show that this is a violation of value because we have a right to attention because attention is a First Principle and First Value—the conversation is a non-starter. And it's actually beginning to be grounded in law. Oh my God! Wow! The Rights to Desire, Intimacy, and Attention

- There is a right to be desired, and to desire, and to respond to desire.
- There is a right to intimacy.
- There is a right to attention.

All of these—attention, intimacy, and desire—are First Principles and First Values of Reality all the way down and all the way up the evolutionary chain.

When they are clarified, they are disclosed as pristine values of Reality, and those values of Reality are disclosed by our core needs and our core desires.

All of Reality desires. At the subatomic level, protons and neutrons desire each other. They are allured. It's 380,000 years after the Big Bang, and they come together, and they create a new immersion called an atom. At that level, there is no split between desire and need. Desire and need are the same. But the desire and need is for a value. And what's the value? The value is this deeper contact and this greater wholeness, which are the basic structures of the Eros equation. The Eros equation of CosmoErotic humanism says that Eros is radical aliveness, desiring ever deeper contact, ever greater wholeness.

That desire lives in the structure of Reality. It lives all the way down the evolutionary chain. It lives in the world of life, all through the levels of life. It lives in the world of the depth of the self-reflective human mind, and all through the levels of the self-reflective human mind. At some place in the human world, desire and need seem to split. We have the sense, I need *this*, but I desire *that*. In the classical life of the egoic human, the separate-self human, that's a given that there is this split. But then, at the higher levels of consciousness, desire and need come back together. You realize, *my clarified desire is my clarified need.*

I have surface desires, but I can clarify my desire. My desire is not to be an incel, for example, or to commit mass murder, or to be madly rude to my partner that I just had an argument with. My desire is to create wholeness. My desire is for deeper contact. My desire is for more Goodness, more Truth, more Beauty, more love. That's a clarified desire.

In CosmoErotic Humanism—based on the panoply of sources and realizations that informed us—we say that Reality desires value. Whitehead, reading a different set of sources, and I guess having his own experiences, came to a similar conclusion:

Reality's appetite is for value. There is a desire for value. That desire is a need, at the most fundamental levels. And that desire and need is a right.

In other words, I have a right to intimacy, just like I have a right to breathe. It's an absolute desire and need. I have to breathe. I can't live without breathing. And I actually can't live without intimacy.

And I can't live without the placing of attention, having attention placed on me.

What we are formulating here is the realization that we cannot just think in terms of value. We have to think in terms of clarified desire that equals clarified need, which generates (points us towards) the fulfillment (the realization) of clarified value, which itself is both a right and a responsibility.

So, I have a right to be desired and to desire. I have a right to intimacy, which might express itself also in privacy. And I also have a responsibility in my desire, a responsibility in my intimacy, a responsibility in my placing of attention, a responsibility not to hijack attention.

The deist language of *self-evident rights* is a way of avoiding explicitly rooting the right in a Field of Value and yet pointing to something that would seem to be intrinsic in nature, in other words, a Field of Intrinsic Value.

HUMAN INTERIORS PARTICIPATE IN THE INTERIOR FACE OF COSMOS

We not only live in Cosmos. Cosmos lives in us and evolves in us. We participate in the Field of Value and therefore can access it. **As such, value which creates rights is rooted in the eternal and yet evolving Field of Value which we access, articulate, clarify and evolve anthro-ontologically.** This is very, very helpful because at the core of CosmoErotic Humanism there is this anthro-ontological clarification (*anthro* = personhood, which holds in its depth the *ontological* = real).

I clarify through my own experience what is absolutely real—not just a surface desire, but my deepest heart's desire, my clarified desire and my clarified need. And those clarified desires/needs are rights.

INTIMACY, DESIRE, AND ATTENTION: RIGHTS AND RESPONSIBILITIES

For example, if I actually begin to realize I have a need/desire for relationship, I cannot be alone. I'm Tom Hanks in the movie *Cast Away*, and I'm on an island, and I've got all my neo-Darwinian issues handled, and I can survive forever.

And yet I find my Wilson volleyball, which somehow made it onto the island with me, and I take my blood and paint a face on the Wilson volleyball—because a face is interiority and I need relationship. I need intimacy. I need Eros. The desire for deeper contact, even if it's only in the realm of the imagination and with a basketball.

And when the Wilson volleyball doesn't quite do it, I throw myself into the Pacific with a two percent chance of survival, because my intrinsic anthro-ontological nature is that neo-Darwinian survival is insufficient, and if my interior can't meet the interior of another human being, I'm going to kill myself. And I am willing to risk killing myself, for the very slim possibility that I might survive the ocean and meet another human being again.

I realize that my nature is that I am both a being of irreducibly unique autonomy and yet I am already in relationship to you. The desire and need for intimate communion **is my interior nature**, my deepest need/desire **and hence my right**. Just like in Buddhism, we talk about an "always already ever-present awareness." There is also an ever always present relationship, right? Therefore, I have both a right and a responsibility towards that communion.

Once every three months or so, I'd have this kind of deep conversation with someone who is particularly bright, who's not fully engaged in the world.

And they would respond to my calling them to deeper engagement with something like: *Listen, it's my life. I have a right to do what I want.* And the answer with which I almost always respond is something like: *Well, no, not exactly that way in Reality. That's not exactly right. You don't have a right to do what you want. That's only an expression of one dimension of yourself. And another dimension of yourself is communion, and you are already in communion with the full range of Reality that is holding you, interacting with you, in conversation with you, in myriad vectors. It is simply an illusion that you are only alone. You are entwined in relationship—in communion, at the level of matter (physics), life (biology) and consciousness every second. And you have a particular responsibility for communion. You have a unique responsibility, a capacity for communion that no one else that ever was, is, or will be, has—other than you. And you have the capacity to ameliorate un-love or loneliness someplace in the world that no one else can do. You have a right and a responsibility for intimacy. It's very beautiful.*

The same thing is true about desire. I have a right and a responsibility of desire. I also have a right and responsibility towards sex, but not with any particular person. **The incel tragedy is to say: because there is a right to sex, I can therefore claim that right from a particular person. That's absurd, the same way I can't claim the right to intimacy from any particular person.**

Similarly, I cannot say I have a right to attention. I'm going to place my attention on you by being a stalker, for example. No, that's actually a violation of privacy. So, intimacy also demands a sense of privacy.

RIGHTS AND VALUES ARE BOTH ETERNAL AND EVOLVING, AND WE CLARIFY THEM BY CLARIFYING OUR OWN INTERIORS

1. The first point is the human being participates in the Field of Value, and therefore we can clarify rights by clarifying our own interiors.

2. The second key point is that rights, like values, evolve, but that doesn't mean that they are not real. We think: *if a right evolves, it's not real.* No, a right is real just like a value is real. And rights and values are both, in some sense, eternal and evolving!

3. One last thought on desire, need, and value: Evolution is love in action in response to *need*. Evolution is love in action in response to *desire*. Evolution is love in action, in response to *value*. It's just a question of where you start, what discloses what. It's very beautiful.

Value is clarified desire. Clarified desire and clarified need equal clarified value.

That's a stunningly important sentence. For years, when we were talking about First Principles and First Values, people would raise their hand and say, *so what do you mean by value?* And gradually this clarified: clarified desire equals clarified value. Once you get that, it's so very ennobling, so affirming of human dignity in a fundamental way.

The core of what we are saying is that need/desire implies dignity, and dignity is an expression of something ultimate—the Field of Value—so dignity implies divinity in the sense of that which is ultimately Real, infinitely powerful and intimate.

Divinity is the *Infinite Intimate*. God is the *Infinite Intimate* (and the god you don't believe in does not exist). The humiliation of our desires, the humiliation of our basic needs, is the violation of dignity and therefore the defacing of divinity.

Evolving anthro-ontology, which is evolving desire and need, also evolves rights and responsibilities.

CHAPTER TEN

FROM VALUES TO RIGHTS

Episode 390 — March 31, 2024

THE MOST MOMENTOUS LEAP IN THE EVOLUTION OF HUMAN CONSCIOUSNESS: UNIVERSAL HUMAN RIGHTS

If I asked you: What is arguably the single most momentous breakthrough of the last 500 years, the single most momentous leap in the evolution of consciousness, which is the evolution of love, in the last 500 years?

The answer would be, at least in great part, the emergence of a new structure of consciousness that existed in certain places before, but became part of the center of gravity of public culture, at least in large swaths of the Renaissance and post-Renaissance, Western world—and it began to ripple into the East as well, although it took more time for that kind of time-bomb to explode there.

And that would be the notion that human beings have rights.

Said slightly differently: **there's a universal set of human rights.**

The single most momentous breakthrough of the last 500 years is the concept of universal human rights which—if you're watching carefully—could easily disappear.

We grew up with that idea. It's kind of our North Star, our axis mundi, the ground which we rested in, the soil that nourished the air of freedom and justice that we breathed

in the West, day in and day out—with all of its tragedy and with all of its weakness and with all of its flaws. **And that idea is being challenged world over.** Putin mocks it. Xi in China talks about the need to get rid of the poison of the Western idea. And the first idea that he regularly cites is this idea of rights, universal human rights. **There's this standing against rights in a fundamental way.** It's Putin. It's Xi. It's Hamas. It's the Houthis. It's Hezbollah. It's Iran. And then there's this enormous world—which is imperfect and flawed—which stands for universal human rights. It's a fundamental idea, even if it's honored in the breach.

Now it's not only that there's these groups that are lined up against the idea of rights. But actually in the Western world itself, if you check the studies all across, you will actually find out that the basic notion of democracy and its sister notion of universal human rights is more and more and more devalued, less and less honored, more and more mocked among the millennial generation and younger, all people who grew up in democracies who actually have no idea what it means not to live in a democracy, have no idea what it means not to live in universal human rights.

You've got this huge, growing mocking of the basic idea of human rights—all by people who are using the sacredness of universal human rights.

Universal human rights means I have a right to a fair trial. There's a universal sense of justice. There's the rule of law. Human rights means that there are a fundamental set of protections that are in place, that are about a universal standard of Goodness, Truth, Beauty—core human rights. It's a big deal. Let's get this super, super clear. **We all live in the context of universal human rights, day to day.** We have access to a court system.

Now our human rights system is massively flawed; if you're poor, you can't afford a lawyer; you don't have access to universal health care; it's a broken system. **But the basic system**—the basic aspiration, the basic demand—**is that everyone is equal under the law and that there's a basic right to life, to liberty, to the pursuit of happiness**—if I can say it in that particular kind of way—to freedom of press, freedom of expression, the right to gather, the right for the state not to have a monopoly on arms. These are all what's called the Bill of Rights. And it's deep. It's deep.

It means that people can't come into your house in the middle of the night and pull you out and kill you, or pull your daughter out and kill you, a.k.a. the way Hamas runs Gaza, or the way Iran is run—where a protest song is written after Mahsa Amini who was killed because she had a little hair sticking out of her kerchief, and thousands of Iranian girls and boys—often in high school—were killed in the last year and a half, because there's no universal human rights.

Friends, just get this straight. If we miss this, we missed everything. Universal human rights is everything. And the assumption that there are human rights that are inalienable, that are fundamental, that are axiomatic is everything. In a certain sense, even the fact that I have to explain this points to the problem. Human rights is everything. It's everything that allows us to live, to function, to breathe. Let's just hold this. It's a big deal.

IF WE CANNOT UNDERSTAND WHERE RIGHTS COME FROM, WE WILL LOSE THEM

Now here's where we want to go. The notion that these rights are real is breaking down around the world. So it's breaking down through all the challenges that I've articulated. It's breaking down through Tucker Carlson meeting with Putin in this embrace without realizing, *No, no, no, this is the man who's killing Alexei Navalny.* This is the man who stands for the kind of state that kills ruthlessly, that kills brutally. But it's not just about Tucker Carlson. It's about the far left; all campuses all across America that embrace jihadi movements, that are about complete destruction of bodies of women that don't follow a certain way of living.

It has nothing to do with colonialism, by the way. As I've said many times, jihad operates in Iraq, ISIS, and in Syria, and around the world, having nothing to do with Israel. Israel is the test case for how we're going to respond to jihad. Israel is an impossible reality.

And of course, our hearts break for the suffering of any innocent victims. But that's what's going on in Israel. How do we respond to a jihad notion that there are no human rights? They don't exist. Which is actually how Hamas has run Gaza. When they came to Gaza and it was run by the Palestinian Authority they basically took sixty, seventy people from the Palestine Authority, knifed them and threw them off of roofs. Let's just understand what we're talking about, as the daughters were raped, often in front of their families.

And again, if you don't get this, we're going to lose it. I just want you to get this. Madly loving you, we have to get this. **Universal human rights is a big fucking deal.**

It took billions and then tens of millions, then millions and hundreds of thousands, then tens of thousands, then thousands, then hundreds, all those gamuts of years to go through all the stages of evolution till we got to a point in global history where, as far as we know, it's the first time that we had a notion of universal human rights. My friends, Romans, countrymen, lend us your ears. It's huge. **It took all of history to get there. And people are ready to not even realize it's there and then to throw it out.** It's a big deal. So where do rights come from. So we've lost the answer to that question.

I can't say this more tenderly, and I can't say it more fiercely. If we cannot understand where rights come from, we will lose human rights.

The universal human rights that are enjoyed in the world today for the last several hundred years in the breach and all of their imperfection, it's such an incomplete and flawed story, but it's the greatest evolutionary advance

193

in the evolution of love that Reality at the human level has ever been able to achieve in history. So if we can't ground those rights in something, we lose. And what are those rights grounded in?

I was reading another article. I have it in front of me. It was the cover story of *New York Magazine* a couple of weeks ago. And it was written by a great writer who I like a lot, Andrea Long Chu. I don't think there's a word she says that I think is ultimately correct in terms of her deepest conclusions. But I think she's a clear thinker within her own frame. I love her writing and I'd love to have dinner with her and her partner, with KK and I. She's just doing a great job and she's honest. Honest is good. She's clear and she's honest. And so she's writing about trans rights. And she basically says, she kind of drops the veil, and she says, *Basically, twelve and thirteen-year-old kids obviously have a right to demand a sex change operation. You can't say there's this and that attenuating circumstance, "They might change their mind. They might recant."* She says, *No. All of that's out the window. That's not correct. They have fundamental rights. Those rights are beyond biology. Biology can't get in the way. Those are fundamental human rights. Period. End of story.* And she says very boldly and very beautifully: just like other rights are not dependent on a thousand extenuating circumstances, so these rights as well are not dependent on all manner of extenuating circumstance.

Now to be clear, that's nonsense. But it's clear. In other words, clarity is a good start. Now what does Chu assume? **She assumes that rights are made up.** Does everyone get this? Stay close for a second. What Chu's assumption is, is that there's no intrinsic, ultimate source to rights. If you don't believe there is an ultimate source to rights, if you believe, for example, *Biology is not coded with value; there is no intrinsic value; all values are purely social constructs*—then you can make up any rights you want. I was just talking to my dear friend, Howard Bloom, who wrote *The Lucifer Principle*, who's a fellow in our think tank and a brilliant thinker. Howard and I talk every other week, I check much of what we're working on in CosmoErotic Humanism against the sciences, and I read the sciences quite actively. I always ask Howard to challenge my science and he always does. And Howard has made me feel good because he says, "Marc, you're a brilliant reader of science," which I appreciate. But I check with Howard in terms of "Am I reading the science or the physics right?" And so Howard and I are talking about rights and Howard just says automatically, "Rights are a social construct." Where did that come from? **Howard assumes, like Chu does, that rights are a completely made-up social construct. So we need to ground rights.**

RIGHTS COME FROM CLARIFIED NEED AND DESIRE

Where do rights come from? So here we go. I'm just going to say it in a couple of sentences.

1. Absolute need, clarified need. *What I truly need, I have a right to.* Absolute need creates rights.
2. Absolute clarified desire. Not desire for a new car, although it'd be nice, but clarified desire, what we call my deepest heart's desire.

My deepest heart's desire is the deepest desire that lives in me when I open up what I call the Eye of Value. **When I see Reality with the Eye of Value—** which is the eye of consciousness, which is the eye of the spirit, which is the eye of love, the eye of contemplation—**I clarify my deepest heart's desire.**

My deepest heart's desire is a right. Why? **Because my deepest clarified needs, before they're a right, they're a value.** My deepest needs are for value. My deepest desire is for value. What is value? Meaning, intrinsic value, real value in Cosmos. What is value? Clarified desire is value. Your deepest heart's desire is for value. That's what Reality desires. Reality desires value. Reality sees with the Eye of Value.

The evolutionary impulse seeks more and more Goodness, more and more Truth, more and more Beauty, more and more wholeness, ever deeper contact. That's the movement of Cosmos to ever deeper value.

Evolution is love in action responding to my deepest and most clarified need. And evolution is love in action responding to my deepest desire. That's the first two steps.

My deepest need and my deepest desire are the same, at both the foundational and the aspirational level of Reality, meaning at the lowest levels—subatomic particles—and at the highest levels—where my Eye of Value is open, where I've clarified my desire. They're the same.

My deepest need and my deepest desire generate clarified value.

VALUE CREATES RIGHTS

When there's a real value, an intrinsic value, you have a right to that value. Goodness is a real value; I have a right to goodness. Wow! It's big. Dignity: I have a deep need for dignity; I have a right to be dignified in my life. I want to breathe, I need to breathe, and I desire to breathe; I have a right to breath. And society has to make sure that I have a right to breath. I have a desire for radical aliveness; I have a right to live a life that's radically alive. I have a fundamental need for intimacy; I have a right to intimacy.

There's cross-cultural research—from both closed and open societies—of a loneliness plague sweeping through the world. I have a right not to be lonely because it's a profound need. It's my deepest heart's desire. And so therefore, as educators, as enactors of political structures, as engagers in economic enactments, as creators of social media, we have a fundamental obligation to allow human beings to fulfill that right.

First, every right is both a right and a responsibility. Next, I've got to be responsible in my exercise of that right, number two. And three, society has a responsibility to create a structure of society that allows us to fulfill those rights.

So for example, Facebook decides we're not going to have a function that allows people to find each other when they're all in the same city to meet up offline. Why isn't that a prominent feature of Facebook? It's not.

For a long time it wasn't a feature at all. I don't know if they've inserted it since. But basically it's a non-feature. Why? Wouldn't that be a great feature?

Wouldn't that do an enormous amount to ameliorate loneliness, to create connection, which Facebook says in its slogans—which are based on B.F. Skinner in *Walden Two*, so they're false slogans—but wouldn't that be a great way of actually creating connection in the world? Well, not for Facebook because then you're offline. Then you're not part of the business model. *Then we can't reality-mine your hijacked attention. Then we can't create a personalized profile about you*—which goes to undermine your freedom of action and reduce you to the lowest common denominator.

It violates your uniqueness—which is another fundamental need; we have a need to be unique and we have a desire to be unique.

Value creates rights. That's huge. It's big.

If you don't believe there's a Field of Value, if you believe, for example, *Biology is not coded with value; there is no intrinsic value; all values are purely social constructs*—then you can make up any rights you want. You say, *Okay, this is a fundamental right*. Why? *Because the social structure of a particular moment decided it was a right*. **Well, that's not going to cut it.**

EVERY RIGHT IS ALSO A RESPONSIBILITY

Every right is also a responsibility. I have a right to be desired because I desire to be desired and I need to be desired. I don't need to be desired in a particular way, in a particular social construct, but I have a need to be desired by Cosmos.

I need to know that I'm desired by Reality.

I need to know I'm desired by my partner.

My partner wants to embrace me. My partner desires to see me walk in. My partner might be a friend, doesn't have to be someone I'm living with. But it means when I get on the phone, I want people to desire to hear my voice. If they don't desire to hear my voice, I'm devastated. I have a need to be desired and I have a desire to be desired. Meaning desire is a value of Cosmos because Reality actually is desire; it's the nature of Reality. Reality has appetite. Reality is desire. That's Reality's nature. Desire is a quality of Reality. Reality is DesireValue. **Since desire is a value, I have a right to be desired and to desire.** Does that make sense?

Since goodness is a value, I have a right to be enacted within the world of the good. It's wild. It's so simple. It's so elegant. It's so beautiful.

Rights are not made up. Rights come from value.

THE FIELD OF VALUE IS UNIVERSAL

If Putin and Xi say, *There is no universal Field of Value, so there's no universal rights*, or if jihad, in the way it's enacted tragically politically around the world, the Sunnis say, *only we are in the Field of Value*, meaning *there is no universal Field of Value; it's just us; God's just talking to us, there's no Field of Value; it's just we who are: value.*

Then you can't have universal human rights because there's not Universal. *Because God only likes Sunnis*, that's why Shiites blow them the fuck up. Or, *No, no, God only likes Shiites*, which is why Sunnis blow them up. **That's not a Field of Value.**

It doesn't matter whether it's a Christian fundamentalist claim or it's a Sunni-Shiite claim. Any claim which says *there's no universal Field of Value, it's just us,* is not in the Field of Value.

Putin and Xi, and paradoxically Iran, Sunni-Shiite, Hamas, Hezbollah, Houthi, et cetera, Christian fundamentalists: **They are not in the Field of Value because the Field of Value is a universal Field of Value in which all human beings participate.**

That's its nature. Therefore, value creates rights, and those are universal human rights. Seems simple, but it's not. It's a big deal. And it's a big deal now.

ACTIVATING THE EYE OF VALUE TO ARTICULATE FIRST PRINCIPLES AND FIRST VALUES

I don't have a right to exercise rights without responsibilities. So I can't say, *I have a right to sex with you, whether you want it or not.* That's not true. That's a disaster. Because there are rights and responsibilities. **Rights are not just *my rights.* It's *my rights in a Unique Self Symphony,* in which everyone has rights and everyone has responsibilities.**

That's what Kant called the "kingdom of ends." Rawls talked about that, this integrated world where everything points to everything and all rights and responsibilities interact together in this beautiful Unique Self Symphony. Without that, there's no game. It's a huge step forward.

If we want to protect attention from being hijacked, it's not enough to write ten books screaming at the tech plex. I've got to establish that there is an Eye of Value. That there are First Principles and First Values.

1. I've got to accept the legitimate critiques of postmodernity of value theory, which were important and good.
2. I've got to respond to those critiques.
3. I've got to articulate a new notion of First Principles and First Values, which are evolving First Principles and First Values.

First Principles and First Values are not fixed, as postmodernity said. They've got a basic ground, but then they evolve. There's an eternal Tao that's an evolving Tao. There are eternal values that are evolving values. That's exciting!

Within the Field of Value, I can access value through the Eye of Value.

How do I find the Eye of Value? What activates the Eye of Value? What's the methodology of the Eye of Value? Desire and need. Desire and need disclose value. It cuts beneath the Eye of the Mind; it's more primal. My deepest clarified need and my deepest clarified desire disclose value. **Desire and need activate the Eye of Value.**

HOW DO WE ENACT RIGHTS?

The very nature of advertising and what we call a free-market economy is about the distortion of desire. Advertising is to confuse your capacity to know your desire. That's literally what advertising is.

So we say it's a free-market economy. Anyone who thinks, for example, the United States is a free-market economy is lying. United States is not a free-market economy. The United States is an economy in which demand is manufactured. A free-market economy means that, as Adam Smith described it, there's a resident relationship between supply and demand. Supply sends a signal into the market, demand sends a signal into market, and there's this conversation between supply and demand.

What we do is we manufacture demand. *Let's create Facebook.* We didn't create Facebook because everybody needs Facebook. No, Facebook was not created in response to a demand. It's a manufactured demand, which uses Metcalfe's law, which is basically, *You have to participate. If you don't participate, you're left out, and you're economically and socially and psychologically isolated because all your friends are in. So you don't really have a choice, you have to be on Facebook*—or whatever it is on social media.

That's a manufactured demand. And that manufactured demand is backed up by asymmetrically powerful AI machine intelligence. That's a big deal. So that's not supply and demand. That's not a free market. That's a market that manufactures demand. And advertising or micro-targeted personal advertising that uses your personality profile is to shape your desire. Now you might think, *Well, we need something.*

We should have consumer information available. That's an entirely different supply and demand economy where you help a person access what their actual desire is.

I'll give you another example. When I was growing up, I remember I was eighteen and I was engaged to a woman from Baltimore. That's a whole story we're not going to tell. But I was eighteen and she was an Orthodox girl, great girl, from Baltimore, Maryland, deep in the Orthodox community or deeply kind of the ultra-Orthodox, more like the Hasidic black hat community. And I remember I'd go visit Baltimore and I was blown away by the fact that everybody got married. Everybody kind of knew everyone else. *Oh, she's not going out. Ah, let's set her up with that guy, or let's set her up with that guy.* Supply and demand were organized and far more effective than our romantic dating system because the families would know each other. Online dating: *We meet people on a dating site. We don't know who they are. We don't know their families. We don't know their values. We don't know anything about them.* And we think like, *Oh, this is going to work,* because we send each other pictures. Really? We sent each other doctored pictures. I mean, it's insane. And we think this is some sort of progress.

But in Baltimore, all the girls and all the boys went out. You might go out with two, three people, *Oh, no, that's not working. Let's try there.* And there was this responsibility of the entire community. It was really beautiful to kind of make sure that everybody kind of got together and that no one was left out when the music stopped. What a better system. And if someone got older, she's just got divorced or her husband died, or she killed him or whatever it was and she's now forty-three. *Oh, maybe there's somebody in New York. Oh, no, no, there's a Jewish community in Malaysia and I heard there's a man who's kind of...* That's how it works. Meaning: *everyone should be engaged in desire and everyone should be desired.* It's based on a system which has a different ethos, and the ethos says *you have a right to desire and be desired.* Now the rabbinic community that enacts that would never say it this way. They don't even realize it. And so it might crash itself and it's got many of its other shadows. It's not that it's perfect. But we don't do that, we've exiled desire to people who evoke a certain reaction in a certain way. That is fucked up. That is fucked up.

I just talked to a twenty-five-year-old kid today who lives in San Francisco. How many people does he go out with? It's the only way he can really go out is go on dating sites because the old gang of college is not there anymore. In other words, these days, a guy can get together with a woman, make a thousand promises. And if she's not from the same community, he can break those promises, walk away for not a good reason and have not been held accountable because he shifted, whatever. And it's not that you can't shift and you can't leave. You can shift and you can leave. And divorce is an option. We don't want to go back a hundred years. But you want to have a sense that, *Hey, there's a Field of Desire and we're all responsible that everyone gets to desire and be desired.*

I'll just give you the last example: loneliness. There are probably six studies in the last three years about loneliness. I got massively interested in loneliness when I was in my early twenties, and *Soul Prints* is really about loneliness. I wrote the early version of it when I was 26, just never did anything with it. Loneliness is non-intimacy. And no one admits loneliness. It doesn't matter whether we're living with someone or not living with someone. That's not the point. How many people reading this experience loneliness in an intense and ongoing way? Woah! But we don't have a design to address that. And that should be a national priority of every country: *Let's address loneliness.* Wow!

And by the way, everyone will admit everything except for loneliness. No one will admit loneliness. But of course, we're all lonely. So it's deep.

We have to create structures in law that create rights.

But that needs to be addressed as a fundamental right.

If we don't think that it's a fundamental right, then we won't get there.

Even the right to privacy. What's the right to privacy based on? We don't know. It's got to be based on something. And by the way, it's probably based on the First Values of Uniqueness and Personhood.

CHAPTER ELEVEN

IMPLICATIONS FOR SOCIAL STRUCTURE: IN DIALOGUE WITH DR. ZACHARY STEIN

THE RIGHT TO DESIRE AND THE RIGHT TO BE DESIRED

Let's say we are talking about the right to desire and the right to be desired. This is rooted in our realization, unpacked in CosmoErotic Humanism, that desire is an intrinsic property of Cosmos. Reality has appetite, and that's an appetite for value. It's what we have called *Eros Value*: an appetite for autonomy merging with communion. One of the things we've said in CosmoErotic Humanism is that in the depths of intimacy and the depths of ecstasy, the old split between autonomy and communion disappears. In other words, you're both most free and most in communion.

That's true in beautiful sexuality, but it's also true in a rave. You go to a rave, you're fully part of the Field of Communion and you are your most free and most individuated.

For a second, let's go back to the realization that the structure of Reality is desire. This is aligned with the Whiteheadian perspective of Reality as appetite, although it is drawn from different sources and realizations. One of the ways we've expressed this, in other works of CosmoErotic

Humanism, is that the name of God is desire. The four-letter name of God that so shaped the Renaissance is the *Yud* enters the *Hei*, *Yah*, as in *Hallelujah*, and then the *Vav* enters the *Hei*, and these are erotic unions which are at the core of Cosmos.

What does that mean in terms of how you educate? What does that mean in terms of how you create society? If that's true, then that means that desire should not be structured through the visual propaganda of society to generate desire only for people that look a particular way: *If your body type is this, then you arouse desire, but if your body type is that, then you don't arouse desire.*

We need to create a field in which we honor all expressions of body, which all deserve to desire and be desired. In mainstream society, the most "beautiful," in a particular embodied way, get to feel their right to be desired, but much of the rest of society doesn't. The amount of times I've talked to people in the inner sanctum, and a woman or a man would say to me, *if only I could actually be desired.* Not because they are pathological, but because we have a right to desire and be desired. Therefore we—as all of us as educators, as constructors of society—need to construct a system of value which generates a wider Field of Desire through its visual structures. That has enormous implications. **If there's a right to desire and be desired, we also have a responsibility to generate a field in which all can be desired in the field by someone.**

A NEED GENERATES A RIGHT, A DESIRE GENERATES A RESPONSIBILITY

We said earlier that at the foundational structures of Reality, need and desire are the same. Between protons and neutrons: need and desire, no distinction. We have to go pretty high in the evolutionary chain, into the world of self-reflective human life (perhaps high mammalian, but for sure into self-reflective human life with a sense of separate self) to make this split between need and desire: *Oh, I need food, I desire a car which*

205

is shiny red. It is this moment in human consciousness which causes the demonization of desire.

We have become alienated from what the lineage of Solomon calls Teshukah: the radical intrinsic desire which is the actual fabric and structure of Reality.

Then, at the higher levels of consciousness, as we said in the beginning of our conversation, need and desire come back together. I can clarify my deepest need and clarify my deepest heart's desire, and they turn out to be the same. When we recognize a clarified need, that need creates a right. Sometimes, like with attention or other dimensions related to the essential nature of our humanity, until that need is challenged we do not need to claim it.

When the need for attention is challenged, when there is an attempt to reshape our very desire for attention, then the need and desire for attention must be *claimed*, and it must be formulated as a right and a responsibility.

When we recognize a need, then we must articulate a right that can allow us to meet that need.

[Zak] In some sense, we might talk about rights as *protecting the powerless* and responsibilities as *holding accountable the powerful*. Need is connected in some sense to being powerless without its fulfillment, and desire is an expression of power, the movement of the evolutionary impulse within me. When we talk not in terms of need, but in terms of desire—desire which is the actual force of the evolutionary impulse, which is filled with power—we recognize the need to generate a responsibility. In other words, a need generates a right, and a desire generates a responsibility. That's a first take on it and is deeply true: needs generate rights and desire generates responsibility. I have desire, but that generates responsibility on multiple levels, because desire is actually power, it's the power of the evolutionary impulse. And a need has a sense of: *I'm powerless, I need you to fulfill the need*, so the need of the powerless needs to generate a protective right. The desire which is powerful needs to generate a protective responsibility.

[Marc] But when you go deeper into desire, desire itself is far more dialectical, far more vulnerable than it initially seems on the surface. In the depth, desire itself both has power and powerlessness in it. On the one hand, I feel the power of my desire. On the other hand, I feel the powerlessness of my desire, this demon hijacking my daemon, acting in me, this thing in me that I can't seem to control or direct. There is far more pathos, far more poignancy in desire than mere power. Desire is not just potency and power, it's also poignant pathos, which points towards not just power, but actually powerlessness.

Whenever we have powerlessness, we need to generate a right to protect it. And when we have power, we need to generate an obligation to responsibility.

THE NEED OF COSMOS WHICH IS DIRECTLY RELATED TO VALUE AND NOT REDUCIBLE TO THE BIOLOGICAL

There is a deeper sense of need in Cosmos, which itself is directly related to value and not reducible to the biological.

Another, complementary way to say this would be that biology itself codes value. There is a shared Field of Value across all words, across all cultures, across all times, even as there is a radical emergence, the evolution of value, which is itself a value of Cosmos. In other words, there is continuity and discontinuity all the way down and all the way up the evolutionary chain.

Need is much more than a reductive materialist random data point of Cosmos.

Need is for survival which means for life. In this context the lineage masters of the wisdom of Solomon talked of divine pathos, which is divine need: **the need of Reality for value, or the need of value for more value**, or, if you want to use religious terms, **the need of God for more God—** God, the intrinsic dignity of value that is backed by the intrinsic nature of the Universe, the Tao, which we would read as the Field of Value. As one master Meir Ibn Gabbai says in the sixteenth century, *Avodah tzorech gavoha*: **Conscious Reality needs your service.**

That takes need to the next level and begins a whole next conversation.

INDEX

LIST OF EPISODES

www.ingramcontent.com/pod-product-compliance
Lightning Source LLC
LaVergne TN
LVHW011911080426
835508LV00007BA/339